Cold As a
Bay Street
Banker's
Heart

Cold As a Bay Street Banker's Heart

Chris Thain

FIFTH
HOUSE

Cover and interior design by John Luckhurst / GDL
Cover and interior art by David Holdsworth
Copyedited by Peggy Lipinski
Proofread by Alex Rettie

The publisher gratefully acknowledges the support of The Canada Council for the Arts and the Department of Canadian Heritage. We acknowledge the financial support of the Government of Canada through the Book Publishing Industry Development Program (BPIDP) for our publishing activities.

THE CANADA COUNCIL | LE CONSEIL DES ARTS
FOR THE ARTS | DU CANADA
SINCE 1957 | DEPUIS 1957

Printed in Canada by Friesens.

03 04 05 06 07/ 5 4 3 2 1

National Library of Canada Cataloguing in Publication Data
Thain, Chris, 1937-
    Cold as a Bay Street banker's heart :
    the ultimate prairie phrase book/ Chris Thain.

ISBN 1-894856-21-X

1. English language—Prairie Provinces—Anecdotes.
2. Canadianisms(English)—Anecdotes.   I. Title.
PE3245.P7T43 2003   427'.9712   C2002-911435-7

First published in the United States in 2003

FIFTH HOUSE LTD.
A Fitzhenry & Whiteside Company
1511-1800 4 St. SW
Calgary, Alberta, Canada
T2S 2S5

1-800-387-9776
www.fitzhenry.ca

About the Author

Chris Thain was born in Vancouver and spent his childhood in Gibsons and Alert Bay, British Columbia; Fairford and Winnipeg, Manitoba; and Peace River, Alberta. A graduate of the University of Manitoba, he was active in the Naval Reserve for three decades and served as the Commanding Officer of HMCS *Chippawa*, Winnipeg's naval training establishment, from 1978 to 1981. He was a high school English teacher from 1961 until 1992, and a member of the executive of the Manitoba Teacher's Society. During the 1980s he collected prairie words and expressions for the first edition of *Cold As a Bay Street Banker's Heart*, published in 1987.

After retiring from teaching, Chris spent seven years coordinating the work of a joint labour/management committee responsible for assisting health care employees and management during the health care restructuring of the 1990s. More recently, much of his time has been spent working as a volunteer in support of the Naval Museum of Manitoba.

Chris and his wife Jean have two sons and a daughter and reside in Winnipeg.

**Cold As a Bay Street
Banker's Heart**

Introduction

I began collecting words, phrases, and expressions that could be considered the property of the West (either as their birthplace or the place they found a natural home) in response to a claim that they did not exist. It was undertaken as a fun exercise with no intention of producing a scholarly dictionary. Such a dictionary is beyond my capabilities, plus the area is too vast, the population too diverse, and the occupations too varied to create one. But it is the prairies and it is distinct from the rest of Canada. Surely there is some fun to be had in looking for a distinctive use of language in the area.

But as I worked with the original publication, I realized how much the language of the West is a language of the past. That sense was heightened when working on this revision. The prairies were settled recently in terms of world history and change has come fast. I was alive when horses were hauling grain to country elevators. I saw hay being pitched onto hay wagons by hand. I played hockey with hockey pucks produced by horses. Now hockey pucks must be NHL approved. Hay is rolled in massive bales that are moved by front-end loaders and grain is transported by semi-trailers to massive steel and concrete, high-volume, regional grain handling centres. The old elevators, so much a symbol of the prairies, are vanishing at an astonishing rate and so is the distinctive language.

The language of the prairies grew out of land settlement and the resulting farms, barnyards, and ranches. It is rooted in survival, animal husbandry, ploughing, and herding cattle. While the same occupations remain they are now done differently. Modern global communication, television, movies, radio, and now the Internet, work against the retention of old pronunciations and expressions, no matter how colourful or succinct.

So perhaps this look at the language of the West has become more history than dictionary, since expecting some of the colourful expressions of our past to continue to be used today is as useless as looking up a dead horse's ass. And that is a shame.

As in

**Alhambra, Alberta;
Antler, Saskatchewan;
Argyle, Manitoba**

Acre

An acre was originally judged to be the amount of land that could be ploughed by a yoke of oxen in one day. That area became a patch of land 40 rods long by 4 rods wide. (Does anyone remember rods, poles, and perches?) By the time the survey of western Canada began an acre was officially ⅟₆₄₀ of a square statute mile, or 4,840 square yards.

While neither originating in, nor unique to, the prairies, there is no better word with which to start a review of prairie language. Across the whole sweep of the three prairie provinces, once you step outside the major urban centres, the terms acre and acreage have traditionally been the basic "coin of the realm." As the prairies were surveyed using a township system that divided each township into twenty-six sections, quarter sections, and acres, most prairie residents will always refer to land holdings in terms of that survey. At times talk may be of sections or quarter sections, but it is the smallest unit of the survey, the acre, to which reference is made most often. This leads to the frequent reference to acreage.

The metric unit of a hectare, being 10,000 square metres, equals 2.4710882 acres, or 2.5 acres for quick comparison. It is difficult to see this unit replacing the acre in common usage as it does not fit the land survey, and therefore does not fit the landholdings. Only time will tell, but it is difficult to imagine this generation's children or grandchildren setting out to purchase hectareage.

As many of the words and phrases in day-to-day use in western

Canada originate with the land survey, for the benefit of those who do not know it intimately from daily experience, the survey and its terms are explained under DOMINION LANDS SURVEY.

All a Steer Can Do Is Try

Steers are castrated male cattle, so, when it comes to mating, to try is about all they can accomplish. Therefore, when asked why you are attempting the apparently impossible, you may well answer, all a steer can do is try.

All Behind Like the Cow's Tail

And where else, pray tell, would you find the cow's tail? While this expression probably predates the settlement of western Canada, it has been a common expression and one well suited to use in farming and ranching country. Children are frequently told to get a move on as they are getting all behind like the cow's tail.

All Humped Up Like a Jackass Eating Thistles

Even those who have never seen it can picture it—just imagine eating thistles! Thistles can, and have been, used for animal feed (see THISTLE TRAMPER), but when they are eaten in the field it would appear to be an unpleasant experience for the animal. A jackass is one beast that will forage on thistles, but it will show all the unpleasantness of the experience while doing so. To be all humped up like a jackass eating thistles is to look absolutely miserable, to be obviously in pain, to look decidedly unhealthy, or perhaps just to be in a strange, contorted position as in "Johnny, sit up straight at the table. You look like a jackass eating thistles!"

All Saucered and Blowed

Once upon a time it was considered quite acceptable, at least for the men of the family when at home or in the company of friends, to pour hot tea or coffee into the saucer and blow on it to bring it to a drinkable temperature. Once saucered and blowed, it was ready to drink. Therefore, anything else that is all ready to go, or ready for use in any way, is also all saucered and blowed.

Anderson Cart

An Anderson cart is, or rather was, a cart made from a cut-down car and pulled by horses. Named after James Thomas Milton Anderson, Premier of Saskatchewan from 1929 to 1934, it originated during the Depression, as did the BENNETT BUGGY. It should not, however, be confused with the latter, which is markedly different in appearance. Whereas the Bennett Buggy was essentially a towed car, the Anderson cart was a cart made from a car chassis with much of the body, and in some cases the front two wheels, removed.

The naming of the vehicles after politicians was not a mark of respect or an indication that they developed the vehicles. Instead it reflected the blame placed on politicians for the hard times of the Depression.

Arrogant as an Elevator

No one who has seen the traditional prairie grain elevator standing tall and haughty, looking down on the surrounding land, needs an explanation of this expression. If you have not seen one, your time to do so is limited as each year more and more traditional elevators are replaced by huge, modern, high-volume flow-through terminals. The new terminals stand out even more on the horizon, but they do not have the same appeal, and arrogant as a flow-through terminal does not have the same ring to it.

Association Saddle

An association saddle conforms to strict standards set by the Canadian Professional Rodeo Association for saddles used in competition saddle-bronc riding. It is a standardized version of the heavy Western working saddle, which, for the Western horseman, is the only true saddle. See also FREAK, PANCAKE SADDLE.

As in

Balgonie,
Saskatchewan;
Boggy Creek, Manitoba;
Balzac, Alberta

Babushka or Baboushka

Once considered the epitome of an absence of fashion, this Central European headscarf has come a long way in recent years. The word in Ukrainian means Grandmother and was, over time, transferred to the traditional head covering of the older women, a headscarf tied under the chin. In western Canada it was originally associated with the Ukrainian culture, but it has evolved from an object of some derision to something associated with cultural heritage. After all, the babushka, or headscarf, is now a functional head covering that may be seen on women of all ages and ethnic backgrounds.

Back Forty

The back forty is a small field away from the farmhouse, but frequently on the HOME QUARTER. If not on the home quarter, it is one particular field, separated in some way from the other land and used for a specific purpose. Forty acres, being one-quarter of a quarter section, is a standard small field, but that field out back will be called the back forty no matter how many acres it actually contains. Here again, metrification got lost. Back one hundred somehow just doesn't have the same ring to it.

For urban prairie dwellers, the back forty may refer to the small patch of land on which they grow a few vegetables, whether it be on their own lot or farther away on an allotment or friend's acreage.

Back Kitchen

Back kitchen is one name for a second kitchen, or wood stove, at the back of the house, usually on a porch or veranda. It was used in summer so that the hot stove did not heat up the house. Back kitchens, often called summer kitchens, are known in other areas, but the extremes of prairie temperatures made them a very real necessity before rural electrification brought the cooler electric stoves and, even later, air conditioning. The prairies are so well known for their cold winters that many people forget that prairie summers are just as hot as the winters are cold.

Even after rural electrification and the arrival of an electric stove, the back-kitchen wood stove continued to be used by many prairie housewives. It took a while before they trusted the temperature setting on the new electric stove. They knew how to get the right temperature in the oven of the old wood stove and so they continued to use it for baking. Using it to bake the week's supply of bread and a few pies had one other advantage. It didn't run up the electricity bill.

Backswath

The backswath is the strip of crop left standing around the fence after cutting a field when the cutter is set to one side, usually the left side, of the equipment. Originally horses, now tractors, move through this strip of crop when making the first round of the field. The backswath can be cut later by going once around in the reverse direction. No, you could not cut the whole field in the reverse direction as that would mean the equipment would be always be moving through the uncut crop.

There is no backswath when using a modern combine or swather as both cut across the front of the machine.

Badger Brush

Badger brush refers to any kind of low bushes or brush. It is a generic term for brush, not the name of a particular type of vegetation. It has been suggested that this type of undergrowth is a nuisance, or badgers the farmer, but it is far more likely that it is simply the type of undergrowth frequented by the animal of that name, just as BUCK BRUSH is brush frequented by deer.

Badlands

Badlands are a true prairie phenomenon found in western Canada and parts of the northwestern United States. They are areas where extreme erosion, predominantly caused by the action of wind and water on the erosion-prone soils in the region, has left a bare landscape marked with strange-looking formations, or HOODOOS, and deep ravines. It is almost desertlike in its lack of vegetation.

The term badlands comes from descriptions of the terrain by early French fur traders who spoke of it as *mauvaises terres à traverser*, or simply, bad lands to cross.

For western Canadians, the badlands is an area in southeastern Alberta, with Drumheller as its unofficial capital. It is in this area that dinosaur bones and prehistoric fossils have been found.

Baldheaded/Bald Prairie

The terms baldheaded and bald have been used to describe the western Canadian prairies ever since English-speaking people have looked out over the expanse of flat prairie stretching to the horizon. It applies especially to the largely treeless southern plains stretching across all three provinces. Many of the trees now seen throughout this region were not there when the early settlers arrived, having been planted by residents over the years as windbreaks. If you think it is a relatively treeless area now, imagine what it was like before all this planting took place.

A number of years ago, in the middle of one of the baldest stretches of the trans-Canada highway, a small lone tree grew beside the road. Some wag, no doubt a passerby from another part of the country, had attached a sign to it that simply said "Tree," as if it needed to be identified.

At one time, the term baldheaded was used as a noun and people simply referred to the baldheaded, without the need to add the word prairie.

Baldies

Baldies are a cross between Hereford and Black Angus cattle, resulting in a black animal with a white face.

Of course, baldies can also be the tires on the old pickup truck!

Bale

A bale is a tied bundle of hay. The traditional rectangular bale of hay, being relatively small, can be picked up and handled by one man. The newer bales of hay may be either much larger versions of the small bales or large rolls. Either one is so big that it can only be handled with power equipment. The large, squared bales stack better than the rolls, but the rolls can be very neatly unrolled along the ground when feeding stock.

Bale the Ditches

Not bail the ditches, as some might think when they hear the phrase, but rather bale the ditches. To bale the ditches is to cut hay in the ditches and highway rights-of-way. Farmers exercise the right to bale the ditches adjacent to their property. While there is no formal agreement with most municipalities or provincial highway departments, the government is not about to complain as every mile (oops, kilometre) of right-of-way that is cut by farmers is a mile less that they must look after. Apparently, in some municipalities, if a farmer does not bale the ditches the municipality cuts the grass and sends the farmer the bill.

Banking

This is not a visit to the local financial institution. Banking is the piling of earth, manure, straw, or other material around the house to a level above the main floor in order to keep the house and floor warm in winter. Even today, with basements and central heating, many people, when shovelling the walks, throw the snow against the foundation to bank the house. Strange as it may sound, snow is a good insulation and will help keep heat in. Manure is excellent for banking as it can generate heat but, for obvious reasons, it should be removed promptly in the spring.

Traditionally, there were two fall jobs required to winterize the house. They were banking the house and putting on the storm windows. Modern insulation, heating, and windows have done away with both of these jobs for most houses, but a few older homes still use the removable second, or storm, window.

Bannock

Bannock is the most common name for a very basic flour and water unleavened bread. Also known as trail biscuit, flour pancake, or other similar terms, it has more recipes than it has names. Recipes range from a simple flour, water, and baking soda mixture to a deluxe mixture of flour, lard (or bear grease), baking soda, salt, water, and secret family spices. Bannock was the basic bread of the prairies in the early days. It could be fried like pancakes, baked like bread, or a blob of dough could be taken up on the end of a stick and toasted in the fire.

While there is a romantic aura about bannock, once they taste it, most people would not choose to eat the most basic bannock if they did not have to, as it is far better at sustaining than it is at improving life.

A number of years ago, Manitoba's Lieutenant-Governor served bannock at his New Year's Day levee. When those attending heard that bannock was being served, there was considerable anticipation of this chance to taste history. However, by the end of the levee there were pieces of bannock in ashtrays, plant pots, pockets, and various other hiding places. The cleaning staff at Government House may well have found bannock under chair cushions for days to come. The general consensus was that it sounded great but tasted awful.

Many people assume that bannock is a native Indian food that was adopted by white settlers. Actually, bannock came over from Scotland where Scottish people had been eating it for generations before they came to western Canada. Many western Canadians with a Scottish heritage may remember their grandparents baking bannock, not out of necessity, but out of custom. In this case, the bannock was often vastly improved with the addition of ingredients such as caraway seeds, not available to those who baked it out of necessity. When someone was famous for excellent tasting bannock, it was usually because of additional ingredients that were a closely guarded family secret.

Barbwire Telephone

During the 1930s and early 1940s, telephone lines did not extend into rural areas. Even if they had, phones would have been an unaffordable luxury on farms and ranches during the Depression. However, while many city dwellers were still dreaming of the luxury of their own phone, their country cousins, with the help of some basic ingenuity, were already talking to one another across long distances. Rural families, wherever barbwire was used for fencing, had one advantage over their urban relatives—they were already linked by miles of fence wire. By insulating the top strand of barbwire from the fence post, that strand became a telephone line across the West. Conversations took place between neighbours on the barbwire telephone without all the problems associated with phone companies, including phone bills.

It is interesting that Saskatchewan, once the land of barbwire telephones, is reported to have led the country in the installation of fiber optic technology for modern phones and high-speed communication.

Barnyard Polka

The barnyard polka is the fancy footwork employed by those moving about the barnyard to ensure that they arrive back at the farmhouse without boots that require careful scraping or removal before entering. See also MEADOW MUFFINS.

Barnyard Savage

A barnyard savage is the calf of a barnyard milk cow. Not one of a dairy herd, but rather old Bossy who is kept for the family milk supply. There does not appear to be any evidence that the calf of the family milk cow was any more savage than any other calf, but that is what they are frequently called. Perhaps it comes from the calf being a little spoiled by the farm children or, more likely, from the way the calf attacks its mother at feeding time.

Bar Pit

Bar pit is a corruption of BORROW PIT that, along with the next word, is heard in some areas of the West.

Barrow

Barrow is another corruption of BORROW PIT that is found in scattered areas across the prairies.

Base Line

Base line is one of the survey terms that has become part of the language of western Canada when giving directions or identifying locations.

A base line is an east-west line from which four rows of townships are surveyed, two to the north and two to the south. Originating at the forty-ninth parallel, the Canada-US border, they form a series of parallel east-west lines, twenty-four miles plus road allowances apart, from there to the northern limit of the survey. For a complete explanation see DOMINION LANDS SURVEY.

Bastard Maple

The names we call the poor old Manitoba maple! More properly called the box elder, this tree is a real survivor and grows well in the western Canadian environment. However, as it is a messy tree, often infested with aphids and sticky with their secretions, it is not particularly well liked. It does, however, grow quickly and can be counted on to survive the prairie winter. For this, it gets called a weed, a noxious weed, or much worse, including bastard maple.

When Manitoba was attempting to choose an official provincial tree the Manitoba maple was proposed. It was suggested that the tree is like Manitobans—you can call them names and do almost anything to them but you can't kill them.

Bay Section

In payment for giving up title to the huge tract of land known as Rupert's Land, the Hudson's Bay Company received one and three-quarters sections in all townships in that area, plus land adjacent to active posts, to a total of 50,000 acres. The sections allocated to the Hudson's Bay Company were usually section 8 and three-quarters of section 16. These sections were leased and eventually sold. However, long after these sections were no longer owned by the Hudson's Bay Company they remained known as the Bay sections.

See SECTION for the numbering of sections within a township. See also SCHOOL SECTION and CPR SECTION. Full details of the land survey are given under DOMINION LANDS SURVEY.

Bearcat

This is a strange and awesome animal! A situation may be a bearcat if it is extremely difficult. Or you may be as mad as, or as miserable as, a bearcat.

Actually, there is no such animal native to North America. It may be a corruption of bobcat or a mixture of respect for the qualities of both the bear and the big cats of the wild. One suggestion has been that this term should actually be bare cat, making you as mad, or as miserable, as a cat that has been shaved.

Bee

This is not the honeybee, but the community bee. The community bee has been, and still is, a very real part of the cooperation that is second nature to rural dwellers. Based on the idea that many hands make work light, bees are a means of assisting each other and the community. There can be barn raising bees, community building bees, or the famous quilting bees, as well as those that are a matter of neighbourly help, as in the seeding or harvesting bee to assist an incapacitated farmer.

Whatever the purpose, the bee is an example of people working together in the traditional spirit of rural living, while also providing an excuse for a scattered community to get together and socialize. In the case of barn or other building bees, they also brought local expertise to help the less experienced.

The spelling bee is an interesting variation on the use of the term, as it is a competition rather than a communal effort. Originally designed to make spelling fun, the spelling bee was actually dreaded by generations of schoolchildren, except, of course, by those who always won.

Beefalo

Beefalo, as you might guess, is what you get when you cross a cow with a buffalo. The cross was made in an attempt to develop an animal that would produce meat more efficiently, matching the size of the buffalo with the meat of the cow. The experiment has not been entirely successful, as seen by the lack of beefalo in today's market, although the cross of the two animals is apparently not difficult to accomplish.

Beef Ring

Before refrigeration was easily available, a group of about a dozen farmers would take turns butchering a steer each week. The meat was then shared among all the families of the beef ring, providing a constant supply of fresh beef to all the members. This is another example of the way in which cooperation, so natural a part of rural life, overcomes problems with simple, imaginative solutions.

Bench

A bench is the geographical feature of a plateau or flat land located between areas of lower elevation, making the origin of the term self-evident. When the people of Ravenscrag, Saskatchewan recorded the history of their area, they chose the title *Between and Beyond the Benches, a History of Ravenscrag.*

Bennett Buggy

The Bennett Buggy was a car converted to a four-wheel, horse-drawn carriage by the removal of the engine, drive train, and windshield (unless the windshield was one of the types that opened). Named after R. B. Bennett, Canadian Prime Minister from 1930 to 1935, this vehicle of the Depression is better known than the Anderson Cart, but served the same purpose. They both utilized a car chassis that could no longer be used for a car, due to a lack of money, gas, parts, or the like. As noted under ANDERSON CART, the name reflects the blame that was placed on politicians for the Depression.

Berm

Many Westerners still call the gravelled or paved width added to a road the berm. While many dictionaries include the shoulder of a road in the definition of berm, most people elsewhere would not associate the shoulder of the road with the word berm. Even in the West the term is now recognized more widely as an artificial embankment.

Bet Your Boots

All of the bet you expressions reflect objects
that are considered to be of great value. They may
include such things as betting your farm, your
mortgage, your bull, as well as the
perennial favourite, your life.

During the Depression, good boots
were hard to come by. As a good pair
of boots was a major asset they were
often carried, rather than worn, to
save wear and tear. To bet your
boots was to bet the thing of most
value that you had with you. This
expression is now widely used, but
it was particularly meaningful on
the prairies during the grim years of
the 1930s and probably originated there.

Biffy

Biffy is, of course, the outdoor toilet. While known far and wide by this
and other names, it has been so much a part of prairie life that it must
be mentioned. No explanation is needed for the terms for the various
sizes of biffy—the one-holer, two-holer, or even the family-sized three-
hole—as these terms were also common across the country. When water
plus sewer or a septic field arrived, a ceremonial burning of the biffy was
often held to celebrate the occasion. In 1967, several communities in
western Canada made the provision of indoor plumbing their Centennial
project, and held a community biffy burning to mark the conclusion of
the project.

Those who have never experienced it cannot fully imagine the thrill
of a trip to the biffy when it is -30°F or worse, with nothing but a thin
wooden wall between you and the wind that is howling out of the
North. You didn't want to take the time to sit and read the Eaton's
catalogue—the standard book in the biffy, which served the dual purpose
of reading material and toilet paper.

More recent generations consider the use of an outdoor biffy, when occasionally encountered at a lakeside cottage or wilderness retreat, as a terrible imposition. However, they have not experienced the joy of the pranks it inspired, especially on Halloween. Of course, the simplest prank was to tip over the building, but nothing was meaner, or funnier, than moving it back three feet. Remember, in those days people moved in the total prairie darkness without yard lights, flashlights, or even, for a routine trip to the biffy, a lantern.

Big Blue Bin

Grain stored in the big blue bin is stored in the biggest bin available—the ground under the sky. In years of bumper crops, when all other storage has been exhausted, grain is stored in the big blue bin on the farm or elsewhere. There have been cases where the main street of the local town has been used.

Big Wheel

To use the big wheel, or to be on the big wheel, is to be in high gear or working as fast as you can. This term comes from the days of steam engines, with their huge wheels and long belts. When the belt is on the big wheel of the engine you are driving the equipment as fast as it will go.

Bill Hook

A bill hook is the very simple, but efficient, three-fingered mechanical device on a baler or binder that ties the knots. The amazing thing about the bill hook is that it has not changed in basic design since it was developed over a century ago. Originally a medieval hooked weapon, the term bill hook was later applied to a heavy hooked knife, such as a pruning knife, and from that to other hooked tools and the hooked fingers of the baler.

Binder Twine

Binder twine is the coarse, strong twine used by a baler to bind, or tie up, bales of hay (or, once upon a time, the binder to tie sheaves). As it is usually in good supply on the farm, it is used for many jobs where something has to be tied together or tied down. The term binder twine, however, never achieved the same figurative usage as haywire—the other all-purpose, hold-it-together, tie-it-down, tie-it-up, make-it-work, make-it-last material. This designation has been more recently achieved by duct tape. See also HAYWIRE.

Bin Sweep

A bin sweep is a vacuum tool used to draw grain from the perimeter of the grain bin to the auger that is removing the grain from the centre of the bin. Anyone who has had to shovel all that remaining grain to the auger knows the value of a bin sweep.

Bismark

Time and TV are blurring many distinctive, regional terms. But traditionally, in Saskatchewan, if you order a Bismark you will get what is generally called a jelly buster elsewhere. If you live in Saskatchewan and need a definition of a jelly buster, it is what you get when you order a Bismark—the donut without the hole filled with a jelly or cream filling.

Bison Burgers

Bison is the correct name for the North American BUFFALO that roamed the Western plains before being hunted almost to extinction. Today buffalo meat can be found most commonly as ground meat used to make buffalo burgers. Fancy restaurants that serve buffalo burgers may call them bison burgers and double the price. See also BUFFALO BURGER.

Bite the Dust

To bite the dust is to be thrown from a horse and therefore, when breaking a horse, to have failed in the attempt. From this, to bite the dust means to lose or to fail at any endeavour. Individuals, teams, or entire enterprises can bite the dust. It may be the child falling off his or her bicycle or Enron falling into disrepute.

Black Blizzard

A black blizzard is a severe dust storm. A true black blizzard is the type of dust storm that darkens the noonday sky with a most ominous darkness. The horror of a black blizzard is not so much the dust that settles out over everyone and everything as it is the loss of tons of valuable topsoil from the farmland.

Fortunately, the black blizzards of the Dirty Thirties have not been seen in recent years, but changing weather patterns and recent drought conditions in many parts of the prairies have raised concerns that they could occur again.

Blade

The blade is the grader that tries to keep the long prairie gravel roads reasonably smooth. Now that much of the road system is paved, or covered in what is supposed to be pavement, there is not so much talk of the blade or PATROL, the other name by which this piece of highway equipment is known. But there are still many miles (pardon me, kilometres) of prairie road that require routine grading.

For the types of roads battled by the blade, see WASHBOARD and CORRUGATED ROAD. See also DRAGGED, as that is what the blade did to the road.

Blankets

In the northern reaches of the prairies and into the North, blankets is often the term frequently used for sleeping bags. If a Northerner tells you to bring your own blankets, you better check to see if what you really need is a sleeping bag.

Blind Pig

This term is known elsewhere in Canada, but it is usually used as a variation for the word bootlegger. A true blind pig is an establishment serving liquor when legal outlets are closed. On the prairies it is most likely to refer to the illegal beer parlour in a dry town, one that has elected not to have liquor outlets of any kind.

As this term predates the use of the word pigs as a derogatory term for police, it does not originate from police turning a blind eye to these activities (something they would not have done in any case). The term comes from the imaginative use of some sort of phoney sideshow as a cover for an illegal operation. The money paid to get in to see the blind pig, the two-headed calf, or the bearded lady, actually bought you a drink when you got inside. From one of the sillier diversions, these establishments became known as blind pigs.

Blocker

If you refer to someone as your blocker you are not necessarily playing football, as this is one of the terms men use when referring to a buddy. While the initial reference to football was facetious, the term probably did originate with the idea of the friend who, figuratively at least, ran interference for you.

The many prairie men who were in the navy brought home the naval expression winger for their closest buddy, making that another familiar expression across the West. (See PRAIRIE SAILORS.) The naval expression of winger comes from the idea of the person who is always at your side.

Block Heater

1. While the term block heater as the device to keep your car engine warm in cold weather is not a purely Western term, its use is far more a part of the prairies and prairie winters than most other parts of the country.

   Our familiarity with block heaters, and the electrical outlets they require, was underlined a number of years ago when a couple from the United States wrote to a Winnipeg newspaper to say how much they had enjoyed their Canadian holiday and their stay in Winnipeg. They commented that they particularly wanted to say how much they appreciated the electrical outlets in all the parking spaces at the Manitoba Legislative Building. They felt that it was such a very thoughtful idea to provide electrical outlets for tourists, as it allowed them to brew a cup of coffee in the camper after seeing the grounds and buildings. The truth be known, someone probably got into trouble for not having turned the power off for the summer!

2. By natural and understandable transition, block heater can also refer to your hat or toque.

Blow a Stirrup

To blow a stirrup is to have your foot come out of the stirrup while riding, especially if this happens when the horse is bucking. The term is frequently heard among rodeo riders, as they are disqualified if they blow a stirrup in a saddle bronc riding competition.

Blowout

A blowout is not just something that happens to a tire every once in a while, but rather a small depression in the ground caused by wind erosion.

Of course, a blowout may also be a drunken party.

Blowup

Also coming out of rodeo vocabulary is the term blowup. When an animal performs a particular type of bucking in which it goes straight up in the air with all four legs stiff underneath, this is referred to as a blowup.

Bluff

Bluff is the word to which many people will refer when asked for an authentic western Canadian word. Elsewhere in the world, and according to the dictionary, a bluff is a rock or cliff face. In western Canada, a bluff is a stand of trees. A stand of trees looming up on the flat prairie does take on the appearance of a cliff face and was, after all, about the only vertical surface settlers were likely to see unless they carried on to the foothills.

Bobwire

Bobwire is the wire fencing with barbs in it. It is correctly spelled barbwire and is pronounced that way by newcomers to the West and a few other fussy people.

Bombardier

The first vehicle known as a Bombardier (pronounced Bom´ ba deer) was an enclosed, motorized sleigh driven by tractor treads and steered by two skis. When the Bombardier arrived on the scene, it provided the first means of relatively warm, motorized transportation in winter over unplowed roads. One can be viewed at the RCMP Museum in Regina.

Bonish/Boneyize

This is a strange expression that many people have never heard and yet it has been reported often enough to warrant mentioning. It apparently means to covet, to wish you had, or to want to borrow, as in "I'm bonish (or boneyize) about your new snowmobile so don't leave it around unguarded." It would be interesting to know the origin of this expression.

Boot

The boot is the bottom of the shaft in the traditional country elevator where the elevator equipment is located.

Borrow Pit

The borrow pit is the area from which earth is being removed for construction purposes. In some cases the earth is, in fact, only borrowed and returned later as would be the case when building temporary dikes during spring flooding. However, it is still the borrow pit when the earth is gone for good as when used in road construction. In road construction on the prairies, the borrow pit is often just the ditch. In other places you will see the earth-moving equipment taking earth from a borrow pit some distance from the construction site.

The term is often corrupted to the borrow, the barrow, or the bar pit. These corruptions of the term may be more unique to the prairies than the original term.

Bottom

The word bottom refers to stamina in a horse. A horse that has good staying power, or stamina, is described as having bottom. Presumably, it was once said that the horse had no bottom to its stamina, an expression that has become shortened to simply bottom. Therefore, the individual with bottom has no end to their stamina or willingness to work.

Bottom Hole

The bottom hole is low gear. If a heavily loaded truck is grinding along slowly in low gear, trying to gain momentum or climb a hill, the driver has it in the bottom hole. Figuratively then, when you are weary and struggling along, you have it in the bottom hole as well.

Bowser

Bowsers were the old gas pumps in which the required amount of gas was pumped up into an upper glass tank marked in gallons and fractions of gallons. The gas was then gravity fed into the vehicle. This happened not so long ago, so there will still be a lot of people who will remember pumping up gas in a bowser. Their children and grandchildren only wish they could buy gas for the same price per gallon that it was then.

Box Social

While not strictly a western Canadian activity, box socials have played a very special part in the history of the prairies. With a relatively small population scattered across a large area, any event that brought people together socially was welcomed. The specific reasons for holding box socials, as well as the rules, varied from town to town and region to region. Generally, however, they were held to raise money for some worthwhile cause and consisted of the women bringing decorated, boxed, picnic lunches to be auctioned off to the men. The men then enjoyed the lunch, in the company of its maker. Local rules allowed, or forbade, a man bidding on his wife's lunch, assuming that he knew which one she had prepared. The highest bids were made by the single men for lunches known, or suspected, to have been made by the single ladies, as this was one of the few accepted ways for young men to meet young ladies.

As the maker of the lunch was supposed to be unknown at the time of bidding, a girl with her eye on a particular fellow would have to let it slip that hers was, for example, the one with the blue ribbon on top. Occasionally, the word got out that the lunch of the most desirable local beauty was decorated in a certain way, and bidding could become a little frantic when a box of that description was presented. Sometimes, however, the information was wrong, or there were duplicate decorations, and some pleased, but bemused, rather plain mother of eight wondered why all the young fellows were so actively running up the bids on her lunch.

Pie socials were also held. Recently, a Winnipeg television news broadcast told the story of a couple who met each other many years ago at a prairie pie social. There had been a mutual attraction but, for some reason, they had gone their separate ways. After many years and full lives they had met again, remembered meeting at the pie social, rediscovered the mutual attraction, and got married.

Brand

Long before we were concerned about brand names of products, we were concerned about brands on animals. Of great importance during the days of open range, and still used today, the brand is the mark of ownership burned into the hide of an animal. Brands are registered with the government and their use is limited to the registered owner. Ranches are frequently known by their identifying brand, as in The Lazy R, whose brand would be an R lying on its side or leaning markedly.

Unidentified cattle without a brand became the property of whoever branded them. It was necessary, therefore, to round up cattle while the young still tended to stay with mother, or at least the herd, cut out those unbranded, and apply the brand. See also ON THE RANGE and SLICK.

Branding, as the act of marking with hot iron, predates western Canada, but it was the West, both in Canada and the United States, that used it exclusively for identifying cattle, not felons or scarlet ladies.

Brat

This is another Scottish term that found its way into the vocabulary of the West. Brat is the scum or frothy surface that forms on porridge as it is being made. Like the crust on a loaf of bread, some people fought to get it and others not to get it. See also PORRIDGE DRAWER.

Bread and Butter Teachers

In small prairie towns in the early 1900s, the schoolteacher, almost always female, single, and from the East or overseas, boarded with one of the community. These teachers were sometimes paid for their labour in produce that they, in turn, passed on to pay for their room and board. More frequently, during the Depression, their only pay was their room and board. Whether paid in produce or with room and board, they were bread and butter teachers. At the height of the Depression it was not a comfortable existence. Teachers of that era have said that they will never forget lying in bed at night listening to the farmer and his wife discuss how much easier it would be if they didn't have to feed the teacher.

While early educators may have been called bread and butter teachers, they were not the only ones to be paid in provisions. Doctors, dentists, clergymen, lawyers, and many others who provide services, have been, and sometimes still are, paid with produce. In fact, not so long ago, (or maybe it is long ago now) the Saskatchewan Roughriders proposed accepting wheat in payment for season's tickets. It was a nice idea, but with today's wheat prices coupled with the current cost of football tickets, if done today they would have to use the football field to store the payments.

Bread and Point

During the lean years of the Depression, there was usually some homemade bread at mealtime but often little, or no, butter to go with it. When you were expected to use only the tiniest bit of butter or, more likely, no butter at all, you were told just to point the knife at the butter dish. Bread and butter, therefore, became bread and point. Prairie grand-parents may still refer to dry bread as bread and point, so today's children probably hear the expression most frequently preceded by the familiar "When I was your age."

Bread and Pullet

Similar to, but different from, bread and point is bread and pullet. Sometimes, during the lean Depression years, a chicken, or pullet, from the barnyard made a welcome addition to homemade bread. However, when the bread was all there was, bread and pullet became bread and pull it, in other words, make do with the little bread that was on the table.

Even if it was not always to be taken seriously, it provided then, and can still provide today, a good answer for the harried homemaker faced with the daily question "What's for supper?"

Both the expressions bread and point and bread and pullet reveal the sense of humour that managed to survive, and helped people to survive, the hardships of the Dirty Thirties.

Breaking

1. The long and gentle process of taming a wild horse, so that it can be used as a working animal, is known as breaking the horse. It comes from the fact that the animal's wild nature must be broken and new habits learned, and involves working with the animal over a long period of time, possibly weeks. First the horse is led, then introduced to a saddle, and then to further weight on its back. Eventually it is introduced to a rider. Finally, it becomes accustomed to a rider and learns obedience to that rider. This results in a trustworthy, reliable animal as opposed to one that is bust. See also BROKE AND BUSTING.
2. Breaking may also refer to the ploughing of virgin sod, an act that was also called busting. See also BROKE.

Break Trail

This is a term of the West and the North. In new snow conditions, or where no trail exists, a traveller on foot, even if on snowshoes, suffers the added effort of breaking down the snow or breaking trail. The same effort is involved in travelling through bush where no previous trail has been made.

If travelers are in a group, the chore of breaking trail is rotated through the group so that each person takes a turn. Even geese know this trick and as you watch them fly you will see the leader break away to take up a position astern while a new bird assumes the responsibility of breaking trail, or (the pun being too tempting), breaking wind.

Breaking trail is now a term frequently equated with the effort required to start any new venture.

Broke

Broke is a word that has to do with both land and horses. While it appears to be in the past tense, it is used for the past and the present. In a strange use of tenses, the horse or the land is broke, or was broke. However, they either will be broke or will be broken and are either being broke or are being broken, as you choose.

Both broke land and a broke horse have undergone either breaking or busting.

Bronc

A shortened version of the Spanish bronco, bronc is a wild, untamed, unbroken horse. Both terms, bronc and bronco, are still used, although bronc is favoured, especially on the rodeo circuit. It is not a breed of horse; it is simply an untamed horse, or one that tries to throw off anyone attempting to ride on its back.

Brownie Points

Most people associate brownie points with positive achievement, the term growing out of the awarding of points for various achievements by the young girls' organization, the Brownies.

But for many on the prairies it has the exact opposite meaning. Brownie points denote demerits, not merits. Railway personnel who broke rules were given demerits that they called brownie points. The term spread to operations where there were detailed rules for work, such as mining.

So, if you say that something you did earned brownie points it may be misinterpreted by some people, one way or the other.

Brushing

The act of clearing land, not as easy as it may sound even on the BALD PRAIRIE, is known as brushing. The term comes from clearing the brush or short growth of bushes, seedlings, and small trees. See also GRUBBING.

Bubbly Jug

Bubbly jug is one of the many terms by which the bittern, properly called the American Bittern (*Botaurus lentiginosus*), is known. It is easily recognized by both its appearance, once you see past its camouflage, and the noise it makes. The names given to this bird reflect these qualities. Bubbly jug is a perfectly understandable name to anyone who has heard one. Its sound is described by *A Field Guide to Western Birds* as a pumping sound or a deep oong-ka-choonk-oonk-choonk-oonk-ka-choonk. See also MARSH PUMP and SHITEPOKE.

Buckboard

The buckboard was a horse-drawn, four-wheeled carriage with a raised seat on a frame of springy boards that gave it a type of suspension. The buckboard, frequently seen in Western movies, is considered the forerunner of the pickup truck.

Buck Brush

Buck brush is a term given to brush and low growth, especially on virgin land. The name possibly comes from deer feeding on this type of growth and being visible while doing so. See also BADGER BRUSH.

Buck Saw

A buck saw is a short, one-person, crosscut saw with an H-shaped handle. The shape of the handle allowed the blade across the bottom of the H to be removed or tightened by relaxing or tightening a connection across the top of the H. You buck wood with a buck saw, but which came first? Do you buck wood because you are using a buck saw or is it a buck saw because you use it to buck wood?

It has also been reported that the person bucking wood with a buck saw is a bucker.

Buckskin

1. Buckskin is the tanned hide of a male deer and yellowish or greyish in colour. It was the main leather of the American frontier and the early Canadian West. Buckskin clothes, like any good leather

clothing, are long wearing under tough conditions. Buckskin shirts and pants were, therefore, valuable possessions in pioneer days when you could not run to a nearby store for a new pair of jeans. Buckskin clothing could range from very plain and functional to highly elaborate and decorated, with most jackets featuring the fringed sleeves associated with such clothing.

2. Buckskin is also a name given to a largely dusky or gold-coloured horse with possible darker points. The basic colour of a buckskin will be lighter than a dun, but darker and yellower than the body colouring of a Palomino. This approaches the colour of tanned deer hide, which explains the name. However, buckskin and dun are merely colour descriptions, whereas Palomino is a breed of horse.

Buck Stove

A buck stove is described in different ways in different areas, but it is most frequently described either as a large wood stove or a wood stove to which pipes have been added to carry heat to other rooms. It could, therefore, be the forerunner of a central heating system before the stove was moved to the basement to become a furnace (in fact, before there was a basement to which it could be moved). The term may be a corruption of either box stove or the Ukrainian *buckshtok*.

Buffalo

The buffalo (or bison) is the great mammal of the prairies. They are now only found in a few herds, such as those that exist under government protection, and in zoos, game farms, and nature conservation sites. These huge creatures once populated the Canadian West in vast numbers, but were hunted almost into extinction for their hide. Canada's largest land mammal, the buffalo was hunted by both the Indians and the early settlers. They killed only as many as they needed and utilized virtually the entire animal. There may have been the occasional hunt for sport alone, but it was the eventual demand for the hides among the white population that led to the slaughter of thousands upon thousands of these great beasts. Their carcasses were left to rot after the hides had been taken.

The Métis hunted buffalo to make pemmican, which they sold to the fur traders. While they may not have utilized the entire animal as the Indians traditionally had done, they were at least using the hide and meat, the two principal parts of the carcass. See also PEMMICAN.

Buffalo Berry

The buffalo berry (*Shepherdia argentea*) is a type of low bush and berry found on the prairies, especially in southern Alberta. While the berry is not particularly tasty, and cannot be used in jams or jellies until after a hard frost, it is believed to have been used to make a sauce to go with buffalo meat. This would account for its name.

Buffalo Burger

Buffalo burgers are hamburgers made from ground buffalo meat. As the slaughter of buffalo is regulated, most meat is not available to the general public. But it often shows up in the form of buffalo burgers at many fairs, exhibitions, rodeos, and some permanent sites related to the buffalo such as the Wanuskewin Heritage Park outside Saskatoon.

Buffalo Chips

Buffalo chips is the name given to dried buffalo manure. It is not just a funny name for the droppings that covered the prairies in the early years—they actually played an important role in the early West. As they ignited fairly easily and burned well, they were used both to start fires and as a fuel. Many early travellers would have been very cold without buffalo chips when there was no wood with which to make a fire.

No doubt many early settlers arrived in Canada familiar with a lack of firewood. However, their relatives at home, who might be burning fuels such as peat, would have been surprised to hear of fires made with buffalo droppings.

Buffalo Coats

Until the late 1960s, several western Canadian police forces, Winnipeg prominent among them, were known for the magnificent buffalo coats worn in winter. Many factors led to removal of these coats from use. A changing society saw more police officers in cruiser cars and fewer walking the beat, and more concern on the part of those officers for quick access to their guns. But the main factor that doomed the buffalo coat was the increasing difficulty in obtaining suitable hides. The event that finally caused them to be removed from use in Winnipeg was the merger into one city administration of Winnipeg and all of its surrounding municipalities. It was impossible to outfit all of the police from the municipal police forces when only Winnipeg and St. Boniface had used the buffalo coats previously.

These beautifully warm coats were made from the hide with the hair intact, meaning that they were fur, not leather. This made them ideal for police on the beat on foot in midwinter in a city like Winnipeg, famous for its winter winds. Their bulk, however, made a chase on foot difficult. The accepted procedure in this case was to drop the coat to the ground and retrieve it later. It seems no one is aware of a coat not being there when the time came to reclaim it. One wonders what would happen today to a beautiful fur coat left lying on the ground, even when it was known to belong to a police officer.

Buffaloed

To be buffaloed is to be stumped, to not know the answer or what to do. This may come from the buffalo's tendency to stampede when surprised and to follow the herd without any apparent thought of its own.

Buffalo Jump

One way that the Indians, and later the whites, killed buffalo was to drive a herd over a cliff or an area steep and deep enough to either kill or severely injure the animals. Where suitable buffalo jumps were available, it removed the danger of killing the buffalo on the run. The area over which the herd would run was carefully prepared and various types of barriers set up to keep them moving in the desired direction. As good jumps were used repeatedly, it was usually just a matter of making repairs. When everything was ready and a herd was nearby, all that was required was to stampede the animals and keep them moving. This was not difficult as buffalo spook easily and naturally stampede together as a herd. The most dangerous job was that of working the bottom of the jump, killing the wounded animals, and dragging carcasses from the pile to be skinned and butchered.

Buffalo Pound

Another alternative to the BUFFALO RUN, when there was no suitable
buffalo jump, was the buffalo pound. This was simply a box canyon, or
similar area providing a natural corral into which the animals could be
driven. The exit was then sealed and the trapped herd could be killed
from the safety of the surrounding canyon walls.

Buffalo Run

A buffalo run was a buffalo hunt, on the run, on horseback. The animals
were surprised and stampeded, with mounted hunters riding the flanks
of the herd. It was a dangerous business, only to be undertaken by
accomplished horsemen and excellent marksmen on skilled horses. Being
a good marksman in this case meant being a good shot with a rifle, while
at the gallop, surrounded by noise, dust, confusion, and the possibility of
sudden death. One false move by either horse or rider and
both were on the ground under the hoofs of the herd.
The Métis were renowned for their skill at a
buffalo hunt.

While taking part in a buffalo run
armed with rifles was dangerous
enough, it was one step better than
using bow and arrows, which
required even closer contact with
the stampeding herd.

Buffalo Runner

A buffalo runner was a horse trained
for, and adept at, the buffalo run.
A good buffalo runner was a valuable
acquisition as it took a special horse, as well
as a special rider, to withstand the frenzy and danger of a buffalo run.
A buffalo runner knew what was expected of it and required little
guidance, leaving the rider two free hands to handle the rifle, or bow and
arrow. A good buffalo runner also instinctively avoided gopher holes and
similar ground irregularities that could bring horse and rider down under
the hooves of the stampeding buffalo.

Buffalo Wallow

A buffalo wallow was an area where buffalo rolled and rubbed themselves, resulting in an indentation in the ground. Sometimes it was around a RUBBING STONE, and sometimes it was simply a suitable area where they rolled to coat themselves with mud as a protection against insects, or just because they liked to rub themselves. The indentations made by these great beasts at buffalo wallows are visible even today.

Bulldogs

Across the northern reaches of the prairies, residents may take perverse pride in the size and viciousness of their biting insects. In these areas, where they lay claim to horse flies twice the size of those anywhere else, these horse flies are called bulldogs. A horse fly can take a sizable chunk of flesh when it bites, and the bite of the bulldog is twice as bad.

Unlike mosquitoes, horse flies, or bulldogs, do not inject a coagulant when they bite. You not only lose flesh and blood to the bite, you continue to bleed afterwards.

Bull Durham

1. Bull Durham was the tobacco kept in a small pouch with a drawstring and used by the cowboy for rolling cigarettes. One of the marks of an experienced cowboy was the ability to make a cigarette, using Bull Durham from the pouch with only one hand and his teeth, the other hand never leaving the reins. Many young boys, and no doubt a few young girls, have spent endless hours and much wasted tobacco trying to learn the skill.
2. Bull Durham is, or was, a polite way to swear, when more direct expressions were far less acceptable than they are now. It is hard to imagine now, but polite ladies even blushed when hearing that expression used as an expletive.

Bull Fries

Bull fries is one term for the cooked testicles of castrated bulls that are more politely called prairie oysters. The term is reported to have amused a visiting veterinarian from Paris until someone suggested French fries with lunch. See also PRAIRIE OYSTER.

Bulling the Cow Uphill

Visualize a bull trying to mate with a cow that is headed uphill. It is certainly not the easiest way of accomplishing the purpose! Therefore, to go about something in the most difficult way, or in a manner more difficult than necessary, is bulling the cow uphill.

Bum Shining/Bumper Shining

This is the act of hanging onto the rear bumper of a vehicle and sliding behind it in icy weather. These terms may not be unique to the West, but the weather that makes bum shining possible for several months each year is unique to the North and the West. It is, of course, a dangerous practice, but every car or bus driver who rages at youngsters hanging onto the bumper must be, deep down, remembering his or her own trips to or from school behind a back bumper. It may be called bum shining even though you may slide on your feet, your back, your bum, or just about any other part of your anatomy.

Bunch of Bales

A bunch of bales is that neat triangular pile of small bales of hay that you may see along the ditches or wherever haying has taken place (see also BALE). This bunch of bales is also called a STOOK, although older residents of the prairies visualize something very different when they hear of a stook. Of course, a bunch of bunches becomes a stack.

Bundle

A bundle is the product of a binder and may also be called a SHEAF. The bundle, or sheaf, was the bunch of cut wheat that was bound once in the middle by the binder. This is an object from pre-combine days when wheat had to be cut, bound, stocked, and then hauled to the threshing machine, or to the farmyard to await the arrival of the threshing machine and crew.

Bungay

Bungay (also spelled Bungee, Bungie, and several other ways), is a term that has come to mean any language that comes from the mixing of two or more languages. Originally, Bungay was the mixture of English, Gaelic, and assorted Indian languages that was spoken by the Selkirk Settlers.

Burn

1. A burn is the deliberate burning off of the land for whatever reason. Brush, or the stubble and trash after harvest, can be disposed of in a burn. This means of removing material from the land is contentious, both from the point of view of good agricultural practice and the danger the drifting smoke can cause if a highway is nearby.
2. Accidental, and potentially devastating, prairie fires are also called burns. While a major burn, such as those known in the 1800s, is now virtually impossible due to roadways and the amount of land under cultivation, they were a very real threat well into the 1900s and can still occur on a limited scale.

    One great burn in 1857 burned over most of the prairie from the Red River to about Swift Current and from below the border to the area of North Battleford. This is an enormous area. The intensity of these burns could be so great that it sometimes took two years for the grasses to recover. While some fires were the result of natural causes, many were set by human beings, either accidentally or on purpose. Occasionally, fires lit to contain buffalo got out of hand. Later, steam engines were a major cause of small fires and at times the CPR, or those with land bordering the track, would plough eight-foot fire guards on either side of the tracks in dangerous areas.

    If you read those wonderful community histories published by many rural areas, often as Centennial projects, you will find constant references to prairie fires and their consequences. Some accounts speak of a wall of fire stretching as far as the eye could see. Such a scene in the pitch dark of a prairie night would have been truly awesome. Just as the dust from the eruption of Mount St. Helens filtered the sunlight and moonlight across the continent for days, so did the smoke from these fires. As you read these accounts, you sense the frustration and despair of those who lost everything, as well as thrill to the intense emotion in accounts that end with a triumphant statement such as, "The guard held!" See also FIREGUARD.

Burnout

No, it is not the effect of too much stress caused by falling wheat prices, rising costs, and unsympathetic bankers—it is a small area of salty soil in a cultivated field. The area may be so small that it is not avoided during seeding, but the crop will not grow properly there, leaving a burnout. Larger burnouts are avoided during seeding.

The problem of salty areas on the prairies comes from leached salts being brought to the surface of the soil and left there as the moisture evaporates.

Bur Under Your Saddle Blanket

Imagine a rider stopping for the night out in the open and throwing the saddle blanket over bushes to dry and air out. In the morning, the blanket is thrown over the horse before the saddle is replaced. Unnoticed, on the bottom of the blanket, is a bur. Once in the saddle the rider cannot understand the skittishness and irritability of the horse until thinking to dismount and check for burs, or other irritating objects, under the blanket.

If someone around you is irritable and cranky for no apparent reason, that person has a bur under his or her saddle blanket. That bur may be anything that is figuratively irritating—something you or someone else said or didn't say, did or didn't do.

The expression is also heard as a bur under your saddle. While a bur under the saddle blanket can also be said to be under the saddle, it is far more likely that the blanket, rather than the saddle, would pick up the bur and carry it to the horse. The former expression is, therefore, probably the more authentic.

Bush

This is an interesting overall term for any stand of trees or shrub, ranging from a small woodlot to a forest. You can go to work in the bush, look for cattle in the bush, or be in the bush any time you go into trees. Whether you go north of the BALD PRAIRIE into the more northern treed area, or into the stand of trees down the road, you are going into the bush.

Bushed

When someone used to urban life goes away from home to work in the bush, or at a bush camp, he or she may stay away from the comforts of home too long and become bushed. This is not the tired or exhausted feeling normally associated with being bushed. This is more akin to cabin fever with the feeling that you just have to get out and back to what you consider civilization.

Busting

Busting is the quick way to break a horse. This is what is seen in the movies when the cowboy jumps into the saddle and hangs on until the horse accepts him on its back. Busting results in a BROKE horse that is undependable and unreliable compared to one that has undergone the more gentle process of breaking. But busting is the only way to make a horse rideable in a short time.

Butte

A butte is an isolated hill or raised area in otherwise flat land. The feature, and the term, are common in the American northwest and southern Alberta. Occasionally, the term appears as part of a place name such as Twin Butte, Alberta, and Frenchman Butte, Saskatchewan.

Buy a Homestead

For ranchers, to buy a homestead is to bite the dust, or to be thrown from your horse. The expression is really a bit of a put-down and reveals something of the rivalry between ranchers and farmers. The expression implies that if you can't keep your seat on a horse, maybe you should give up riding and become a farmer now that you have bought a homestead face first. See also TOOK A HOMESTEAD.

Buy the Farm

1. To buy the farm is to die. This apparently comes from the feeling that the only time you will be able to have your own land, bought and paid for, is when it is your grave. This is not to be confused with the expression BUY A HOMESTEAD.

2. To buy the farm also means to be badly bested in a deal. To say "He bought the farm that time," means that someone came out of whatever it was very badly indeed. This expression may reflect the idea of being "killed" in a deal, or the feeling of many farmers that, as much as they love the land and the work, buying a farm is often not the best of business deals.

As in

*Carey, Manitoba;
Carcajou, Alberta;
Cutknife,
Saskatchewan*

Caboose

The first association with caboose for most people will be the once familiar tail-end car of a freight or work train. However, the word has a much wider use. The bunk cars used by work crews on the railway, and elsewhere, are also cabooses. The original cabooses on the prairies were probably the bunkhouses on runners that could be pulled from worksite to worksite. These uses of the word may not be unique to the West, but apparently what is unique was the use of the word for a large horse-drawn sleigh. These sleighs, which were not necessarily work sleighs, were completely closed in and, in some cases, even had stoves to provide heat while travelling.

The replacement of the red train caboose with a small electronic sensor caused for many, a safety concern. But for many more, it was the loss of a very real part of the prairie scenery. Not only could you wave to the engineer and fireman as the train went by, but, if you waited long enough, you could wave to the conductor sitting in the cupola (CROW'S NEST) of the caboose.

Cackleberries

Cackleberries are, of course, eggs—common hens' eggs. Those who do not understand the reasoning behind this expression should stand in a henhouse for a while.

Calf at Foot

A calf at foot is a calf that is still very much with its mother and very much underfoot as it attempts to stay as close as possible to her udder. It is this common expression, under foot, that has become at foot. The small child that is clinging to its mother's skirt, hanging on and not allowing her to take a step, is behaving like a calf at foot. A mother may say, "I couldn't get anything done this morning because Matilda insisted on being a calf at foot."

Calgary Redeye

The mixture of tomato juice and beer, which began in southern Alberta and has spread far and wide, is known as Calgary Redeye, or simply Redeye. Those who do not appreciate this use of tomato juice, as they might in a Bloody Mary, are more likely to refer to the practice as a bloody waste of beer! See also TWO AND A JUICE.

Californian Widow

Most people have heard of golf widows and similar types of widows. Dating back to the days of the California gold rush, a Californian widow refers to a woman whose husband has left home for a long period of time to seek his fortune elsewhere, leaving his wife to tend the home and family. While originating in the United States, it is a term that found a home on the Canadian prairies. During the Depression many men left home in a desperate effort to find work, leaving behind innumerable Californian widows.

Can Be Ridden But Not Spurred

There are horses that will allow you to ride them, but react violently if you dare to put the spurs to them. The expression was quickly transferred to people to describe those who are generally cooperative, hard-working individuals who will take direction, but who bristle and kick back at any attempt to order them about or force them in any way. Unfortunately, modern slang makes the use of this very meaningful expression inappropriate today.

Candy Pail

The candy pail is a euphemism, along with the more common thunder mug, for chamber pot, a very common object before indoor plumbing, and still in existence in a few places. At one time, candy was commonly bought in small tin pails and it was the use of these pails as chamber pots, and a sense of humour, that led to the expression. Be it candy pails or honey wagons, there is certainly a common theme of making references to bedpans and biffies.

The term honey wagon apparently came out of the American Civil War and has been used all across the continent. Therefore, despite its routine use in the West, it cannot be counted as a Western expression.

The thought of candy pails and thunder mugs brings to mind all the expressions that come from the use of chamber pots. "They don't have a pot to pee in" was a level of poverty only exceeded by "They don't have a pot to pee in or a window to throw it out." Or maybe your area added the more sophisticated phrase, "Or a piano to put it on!"

Canter

A canter and the equipment used, the CANT HOOK, are Canadian terms that many claim to have been more common in Western lumbering than elsewhere. (Yes, there was a lot of lumbering in parts of the West but not, of course, on the BALDHEADED.) The canter stood beside the log as it was fed into the saw at the lumber mill and, using a cant hook, turned the log to ensure that the largest possible amount of usable lumber was obtained from the log.

Can't Hit the Broad Side of a Barn

This expression usually ends with a number of paces added, as in, "He can't hit the broad side of a barn at forty paces." While the expression originated as a description of terrible marksmanship with a gun, it is now used to indicate the inability to hit any form of target with any type of missile.

Can't Hit the Bull in the Arse With a Scoop Shovel

This expression takes CAN'T HIT THE BROAD SIDE OF A BARN one step further. It refers to both a broad target and a wide weapon. While often used to describe an absolutely terrible marksman, it can also be used to describe someone who is totally uncoordinated. This could refer to the person who is a candidate for the more recent saying, "Can't walk and chew gum at the same time."

Cant Hook

A cant hook is a log-turning device, properly called a peavey, but more commonly known as a log dog. It features a hinged, rather than fixed, hook on the end. When the handle is raised, the hook bites into the log, but releases quickly when the handle is lowered.

Carrol

A carrol, or carol, is a small two-seater sleigh, an obviously Anglicized version of the French word *carriole*. It is another example of borrowed language—what some see as a threat to the purity of language and others see as its living quality.

Carter Disk

The Carter Disk, sometimes called an indented disk, and really more of a drum than a disk, is a machine used to clean, or separate, seeds on the basis of size and weight. It is a long drum with indentations on the inside that rotates around a V-shaped trough down the centre. The seeds being cleaned enter the bottom of the revolving drum and, by centrifugal force and the indentations in the drum, are carried up the side of the drum and dropped into the central trough from which they are drawn off by an auger. Seeds of a wrong shape, size, and/or weight, fail to climb the side of the drum and fall back to the bottom.

The rotation speed of the Carter Disk controls the weight of seed lifted to the trough, while the indentations add a control to size and shape. Each type of seed to be cleaned, therefore, has its own Carter Disk. The final control on the purity of the cleaning process is obtained by tilting the edge of the central trough up or down. The higher the edge of the trough, the cleaner the final product, but that purity comes at the price of good seed that fails to make the trough. The skilled operator makes the adjustment that allows maximum seed to be retained with minimum impurities.

The Carter Disk is so called because it was developed in Winnipeg by the Carter Implement Manufacturing Co.

Cart Wheel

As the largest of Canadian coins, the silver dollar was commonly called a cart wheel.

Cast

The term cast is most commonly associated with cows, but can apply to any animal that cannot, for whatever reason, regain its feet. While the term is used in this manner far beyond the prairies, it is more common in the extensive farming areas of the West, which leads to a wider meaning unique to the prairies.

In many areas of the West, the term has been applied figuratively to people who are so absolutely tired and weary that, having sat down, they feel that they will never get to their feet again. In this case they may claim to feel cast or like a cast cow.

Catch Colt

A catch colt is a colt with an unknown sire. This, of course, is not desirable when animals are being carefully bred. Even when breeding is not of utmost importance, farmers usually know which stallion is responsible for which colt, so a catch colt is not all that common.

Again, the term can be applied euphemistically to the human condition. It sounds so much nicer to say that he is a catch colt than to say that no one, except perhaps his mother, knows the identity of his father. A catch colt, like a CATCH CROP, may have been unexpected, but happened for a reason.

It is interesting that the term only applies to the colt, or male, without any similar expression noted for the filly with the unknown sire. Perhaps catch filly just does not have the same alliterative ring to it.

Catch Crop

Occasionally, land left fallow seeds itself from seeds accidentally, or naturally, dropped from the previous year's crop, or blown in or transported in from other fields on farm vehicles. This unexpected crop is called a catch crop or VOLUNTEER CROP. Both terms are used interchangeably, but if a distinction is to be made it may be that the catch crop grows on field left fallow or unseeded while a volunteer crop grows in among a seeded crop.

Neither terms can be applied to alfalfa, which is a true perennial and will grow year after year.

Cattle/Cow Gate

A cattle gate, or cow gate, is distinct from a CATTLE CROSSING as it is the gateway in a path rather that a gateway in a road. Instead of placing a gate in the opening in a fence, a short length of fencing is placed parallel to the fence outside, and extending a couple of feet on either side of, the opening. A person can walk through the opening, turn right or left, and be through the fence without opening and closing a gate. However, the space between the two fences is narrow and the turn required is too tight for cattle to negotiate, keeping them contained within the fence.

Cattle Crossing

While not entirely unique to the West, the cattle crossing is an ingenious device that is, by use, part and parcel of the Western experience. Where a road passes through a fenced area the roadway is replaced by poles, narrow timbers on edge, or metal strips running across the road over a dug out area. The gaps between the strips are such that the combination of cross strips and spaces allows vehicles and people to pass through, while cattle cannot as their hoofs will not allow them to walk on the surface.

The cattle crossing provides an effective barrier without requiring a gate that has to be opened and closed when passing through with a vehicle. In some areas, this type of cattle crossing is called a TEXAS GATE.

Caught Using Purple

To help ease the strain on farm budgets, the prairie provinces allow farmers to buy gas for farm equipment which is exempt from certain road taxes. In an attempt to prevent the illegal use of this cheap gas in family cars, the gas is dyed purple. Police in rural areas routinely check cars on the highway for purple gas. Checking the colour of the gas was far easier in the days when cars had glass sediment bowls, or site glasses, as part of the fuel system. Today, police carry a siphon that draws a small amount of gas from the gas tank so that the colour can be checked. To be caught using purple was therefore, literally, to be caught using purple gas in a vehicle off farm property.

Some farmers, or at least their teenagers, considered the use of purple gas off the farm to be perfectly acceptable, unless you got caught. Therefore, the expression "caught using purple" became generalized to mean being caught doing something where it was generally believed that the crime was not the illegal action, but being caught.

If caught using purple gas on the highway, you might say you have just run out of gas and stopped at the last farmhouse to borrow enough to get to town and, wouldn't you know it, all they had was purple! Even in the rare case when it is true, the police never have, and never will, buy that excuse.

Cavvy

A cavvy is a spare horse taken along when working cattle over a long period of time, as in a cattle drive, to provide a rest for your main horse. As with so many terms, this one can also be used figuratively for a backup, or spare, to the main or usual object of use.

Cayuse

Originally a cayuse was an Indian pony. From there the term was used to refer to any wild horse or mustang. Later it became customary to call any horse a cayuse.

The Cayuse Indians lived in the area that eventually became the states of Washington and Oregon. As a result of contact with Spanish explorers in the late 1500s, they acquired horses which they bred to create the type of horse that took their name.

CBC Sunshine

CBC sunshine is the rain that pours down an hour or so after a CBC radio weather forecast states that it will be sunny. In other words, it looked a little grey, but the radio said it was going to clear up, so you went to work and just had time to get the equipment running and nicely onto the field when it began to pour.

At least this is one time the forecaster doesn't take the blame for the inaccuracy of the forecast. The messenger is blamed instead.

Cement Pigs

Pigs, being very nervous during transportation, tend to make quite a mess in the truck taking them to market. The problem is not just the mess in the truck, but also the loss of weight. The truck can be hosed out (although an aroma persists), but the loss of weight means loss of money at the market. You could not get away with it today, quality controls being what they are, but there was a time when a farmer might add a scoop shovel of Portland cement to the pigs' final feeding prior to shipping. The cement did a marvelous job of constipating the pigs, resulting in a cleaner truck and, the main consideration, more weight retained at the scales.

What would you call pigs treated this way? Cement pigs, of course.

Central Canada

Many Westerners, particularly Manitobans, cringe when broadcasters refer to southern Ontario as central Canada. The only place that could justifiably call itself central Canada would be Manitoba. After all, it is central by location as well as by shape. It is the Keystone Province and the longitudinal centre of Canada (96° 48′ 35″ west) crosses the trans-Canada highway just east of Winnipeg.

Most Westerners do not use the term central Canada at all. For them there are five areas of Canada. They are the North, the East Coast (or Maritimes), the East (Ontario and Quebec), the West, and the Coast. Note that the Coast is always the West Coast.

While acknowledging that all directions are relative, Westerners tend to believe that Easterners see things only from their relative perspective, no matter with whom they are dealing. And the Eastern press doesn't help. At the same time as a Toronto-based "national newspaper" was defending its national outlook against charges that it was only a Toronto newspaper distributed nationally, it ran an article that stated, "The physicians are needed in northern communities that include Dryden, Elliot Lake, Hearst, Geraldton, Hornepayne and Fort Frances." These six so-called northern communities are all south of Winnipeg, Regina, and Calgary. Three of them are south of Vancouver. If those cities are then viewed as northern cities, how on earth does that paper view the likes of Fort Simpson, Yellowknife, and Churchill?

Chaps

Old-timers will tell you that this word is properly pronounced shaps. They are the heavy leather leggings worn by cowboys, or for that matter, anyone who has to spend much time on horseback. They cover the legs in front and on both sides, and come up to the waist only as far as is required to keep them on, so they do not have a seat in them. They serve the dual purpose of protecting the inside of the leg from chaffing against the saddle and the outside of the leg from low branches and brush. As chaffing is the main concern, chaps are made from leather heavy enough not to crease or bunch up as the rider's legs rub up and down on the sides of the saddle.

At one time bearskin was considered the best leather for chaps, both in terms of function and fashion.

Chicken Feed

Chicken feed, as well as being something fed to chickens, is small change, relatively small amounts of money, or small amounts or values of other goods. In whatever connotation it is used, chicken feed is not worth worrying about.

As commercial chicken feed is not cheap, the expression must have started when the only food fed to the chickens, other than that scratched in the barnyard, was scraps.

Chikay

Chikay, pronounced and sometimes spelled chickeye, is another of those borrowed, but slightly mutilated words from another language, once again from Ukrainian. It means wait or stay and, in English, it is usually used to mean wait for me, stay there, or stay there until I come.

Repeated sharply, it is a warning not to move, for whatever reason.

Chinese Cafe

The Chinese cafe is such a part of every Western community that it must be included when dealing with the language of the West. Virtually every Western town has, or until very recently had, a Chinese family that ran a cafe. This phenomenon was examined in a CBC documentary in the 1980s.

These cafes were, and frequently still are, eighteen-hour-a-day, seven-days a week, fifty-two weeks of the year operations. If you find yourself in a small town on the prairies on a Sunday, Christmas Day, Labour Day, or any other day of the year when everything else is closed up tight, you can probably get a meal at the Chinese cafe. Long before the cities had their chains of convenience stores, western Canada had its network of Chinese cafes that provided their communities with much the same service in conjunction with a restaurant.

Why the Chinese tended to spread themselves out in the lonely isolation of one family to a community across the West, rather than gathering together in areas as most other ethnic groups tended to do, is not entirely clear, but hundreds of Western communities are very thankful that they chose to do so.

Chinking

Being both noun and verb, this is both the material used to fill, and the act of filling, the gaps, or chinks, between logs in a log cabin or the cracks in any other structure. It could be mud, manure, moss, or many other substances or combinations of substances. There are some reports that a few hardy souls considered chinking cabins in winter a sign of physical weakness, but the vast majority considered it a necessity.

Any crack may be chinked. One city resident, in an older house, reports chinking the cracks in the foundation of his house with dryer lint.

Chinook

1. While residents of Saskatchewan and Manitoba sometimes speak of a chinook when unseasonably warm air moves in during winter, a true chinook is only experienced in parts of Alberta, particularly the Calgary area.

    A chinook can raise the temperature dramatically in an hour or less and decrease it just as quickly. There are reports of the temperature rising 75 Fahrenheit (or 42 Celsius) degrees in one hour. It is the result of warm, moist, Pacific air rising over the Rockies and then pushing down and out onto the plains. As it moves up the western slopes, the moisture condenses and falls as rain, releasing latent heat that warms the air. This relatively warm, and now dry, air flows down the eastern side of the mountain and is further warmed by compression. If this air, which is now relatively hot, pushes under the colder air to the east of the mountains, the chinook occurs.

    The name is that of the Chinook Indians, but there are several stories to explain how it came to be attached to this warm wind. One explanation is that the term was first used at Fort Astoria. This explanation states that as the warm wind was coming from the direction of Camp Chinook, also named after the Chinook Indians, it became a chinook wind.

2. The term Chinook is also used occasionally to refer to a combination of Indian and English—a type of pidgin English.

Chinook Arch

The atmospheric conditions that produce a chinook may also produce a high arch of clouds over the mountains through which the wind is travelling. The sight of this arch of cloud, or chinook arch, is often the first indication that a chinook is approaching.

Chipwageese

Chipwageese is a Northern term for a potent form of home brew. Making chipwageese is not a long-term project as this is not an aged product by any stretch of the imagination. In fact, it is ready in a matter of a few days. It is sometimes also called by that catch-all term for strange and potent drinks—hootch. It is sometimes called moosemilk, although true moosemilk is a very specific drink. See MOOSEMILK for the proper contents of that drink.

Chokecherry

Native to North America, the chokecherry (*Prunus virginiana*) with its small dry berries, is found extensively on the prairies. While berries eaten directly off the shrub are generally considered unpleasant, chokecherry jam, jelly, and wine can be very good.

Chokecherry Farmer

This is one of those terms, usually considered somewhat derogatory, that may be applied to farmers. Actually, the term is usually applied to a farmer who is having difficulty making a go of it. These days that could apply, unfortunately, to a lot of them.

Chop

Chop and chopping have nothing to do with wood. Chop is the product of a grain crusher. The grain crusher is not unlike a small flour mill, consisting of two rough wheels between which the grain is rubbed. The grain crusher, however, does not reduce the grain to flour. It removes the husk and slightly crushes the kernel. The purpose is to make the grain more digestible for the cattle as, without crushing, most grains would pass through the animal virtually undigested.

Chuck

Chuck is the old Western term for food or meals. The term, by itself, is not as familiar as that of chuckwagon, the mobile kitchen of the range. Today, the chuckwagon is seen primarily at the rodeo in the chuckwagon races.

Cinch Hooks

A cinch is a wide strap that goes under the horse's belly to hold the saddle in place. Cinch hooks might reasonably be supposed to be hooks to fasten the cinch, but they aren't. Cinch hooks are your spurs, as occasionally, when riding a bucking horse, a spur gets caught in the cinch, something that definitely does not improve riding style!

Claim Jumper

For the western Canadian, a claim jumper is not the gold rush individual who mines another's legally staked claim, but rather someone who settles on land that is not theirs. A squatter is a form of claim jumper but, if a distinction is to be made, it would be that the claim jumper will try to claim the land as theirs, while the squatter just lives there without any real concern for who the legal owner might be.

Clean Meal

The harried homemaker loves a clean meal. This is a term reportedly used in some areas to indicate a meal that is cooked by someone else—all you have to do is eat and enjoy it. Therefore, clean meals usually involve visits with neighbours and friends. The term is not usually applied to a restaurant meal as it originated with those for whom there was no restaurant.

For homemakers on the farm, who have few breaks from planning and preparing three meals a day, and for whom ordering in is not a possibility, being invited to a neighbour's home for a clean meal is very welcome.

Codland

Codland is a Westerner's term, meant affectionately of course, for Newfoundland. Codlanders are, therefore, those who come from Codland.

No doubt many Newfoundlanders wish that the term could be as meaningful today as it was in the past.

Cold as a Bay Street Banker's Heart

This expression needs no explanation to anyone, anywhere, but especially not to Westerners who feel, not without some justification, that the financiers of Bay Street cannot see beyond the suburbs of Toronto, and have no heart or compassion anyway.

The term is sometimes heard as "cold as a Bay Street bastard's heart," but it makes little difference to many farmers who, lately at least, see little difference between bastards and bankers, especially if their offices, or corporate headquarters, are in Toronto and the farm line of credit is up for review.

Colt

A colt is a young male horse. Young usually includes any horse under four years of age.

Combine

A combine is a machine that can combine the function of a reaper, or swather, and a thresher. The combine may pick up the swathed crop, separate the grain from the chaff and straw, store the grain until it is passed to a grain truck alongside, and disburse the chaff and straw back on to the ground. When straight combining, the combine also cuts the crop instead of picking up a cut swath.

The modern combine is an extremely technical, complex, and very expensive piece of equipment. The cab, for the uninitiated, is an intimidating place with multiple controls, lights, dials, and warning indicators, not to mention the possibility of air conditioning, sound system, and CB radio for contact with the farmhouse, trucks, and other equipment. Today, it may even contain a GPS receiver to record its exact position on the field at any time.

A full-sized modern combine with all the bells and whistles costs in the neighbourhood of $250,000. Put another way, that is a quarter of a million dollars for one piece of farm equipment.

Comforter

Western Canadians are, of course, familiar with the term quilt. Quilting bees have been, in fact, very much a part of Western living. There is another term for a quilt, however, which appears to be used far more on the prairies than elsewhere. That term is comforter. On a bitterly cold night when you wrap one around you as you sit in front of the fire, or gratefully slide beneath one into bed, there can be no better descriptive term than comforter.

Common

To be common in the West is simply to be like everyone else, no worse and certainly no better. This is not the same meaning as in many places where to call someone common means that they are vulgar or immoral. It is not an insult in any way, and many would consider it to be a compliment, to be called common, or just plain folk.

Co-op

While both purchasing and marketing cooperatives are known across the country, and in fact were first seen in Canada in the Maritimes, cooperative marketing is nowhere more developed or important than in the grain marketing industry of the prairies.

Cooperative grain marketing started to take shape in 1906, with the entry of the Grain Growers' Grain Co. into the Winnipeg Grain Exchange. This company took over the elevators built by the Manitoba government and then, in 1917, amalgamated with the Alberta Farmers' Cooperative Elevator Co. to form United Grain Growers, known to this day across the West simply as UGG. This company, together with the Saskatchewan Cooperative Elevator Co., handled up to one-quarter of Western grain at that time. The provincial pools started soon after and, from then on, the cooperative marketing of Western wheat has been a fact of life.

Cooperative purchasing, ranging from co-op implement dealerships to co-op grocery stores, is also well known on the prairies, but its success cannot rival that of cooperative marketing. Cooperative financial services, or credit unions, form the third, and very successful, part of prairie co-op services.

Corduroy Road

A quick way to create a road over swampy land, or ground that is impassable when wet, is simply to cut small trees and lay them side by side across the roadway. This creates a very rough but effective wooden road. It was sometimes also called a CORRUGATED ROAD, although the latter term usually applies to something different.

Correction Line

Directions on the prairies are frequently given in terms of the correction line. While correction lines are fully explained under DOMINION LANDS SURVEY, it must be noted here that the north-south divisions between townships are true meridians of longitude and therefore converge northwards. To adjust for this convergence, the dividing line must be adjusted slightly after every four townships.

The correction line is the continuous east-west line, midway between base lines, on which these corrections take place. They are identifiable by the jog in the north-south road as the road allowance shifts to the new township division. That jog in the road gives an easily identifiable location on both the north-south and east-west roads following the road allowances.

Corrugated Road

Sometimes a corrugated road is confused with a CORDUROY ROAD. However, corrugated road properly applies to a gravel road that has developed ridges running from side to side resulting in a rough ride, not a road made of logs. Those patches of corrugation on the road start from one bump and spread down the road as a vehicle's bounce from the first bump creates the next ridge. Continuing traffic deepens and extends the corrugation. The condition will be known wherever there are gravel roads, but nowhere in Canada are there so many miles (oops, sorry, kilometres) of rural road as on the prairies.

Patches of deliberate corrugation are now built into paved highways to act as wake-up, or rumble, strips that warn of a stop sign. They can also warn a driver who drifts onto the shoulder of the road. But the real corrugated road is found in those patches in the gravel road leading to the highway, which test the most elaborate vehicle suspension system.

Cottonwood

While poplar trees of various types throughout North America are frequently called cottonwoods, the name seems to be used more often in the West. Perhaps it was Hollywood's fondness for hanging the rustler from the cottonwood that has given a Western connotation to the word for most people.

Coulee

A coulee, with the accent on the first syllable, is a wide ravine or valley. Often a mile or more wide, it may have a river in it, but is usually dry except at runoff time. This led to it being called a run in some places.

When the land formations between coulees are benches, the topography, such as that east of the Cypress Hills, may be called bench coulees.

Just by way of interest, in the 1980s Manitoba named a coulee after a man named Dooley. The result, of course, is a place officially called Dooley Coulee—and that's the truth!

Coulter

A coulter is a device to assist in ploughing a straight furrow. Made in various fashions for different types of ploughs, it attaches to the plough and rides in the previous furrow to keep the plough moving parallel to that furrow. Provided the first furrow is straight, the remaining furrows will also be straight.

It is a device of the past, as it was for use with a small horse-drawn plough that was easily thrown off-line. However, whether using old foot burners or modern gang ploughs, farmers have always been judged by the straightness of their furrows. See also PLOUGH A CROOKED FURROW.

Country Alliance
or Country Wife

When a man, either from the East or from overseas, went West, or "into the country," he was gone from home for months or years at a time. Whether or not he had a wife at home, it was not unusual for him to take a companion for the time that he was away. Both parties understood that it was a temporary arrangement that was terminated when the man went home. Such an arrangement went by the name of country alliance. The woman was, therefore, the country wife and the couple was spoken of as being married in the custom of the country.

Actually, since the society at the time was male dominated, the women had little say in the matter. To obtain a country wife, it was only necessary to reach agreement with the woman's father, who might require a suitable gift before agreeing. The woman was usually Indian. She may, or may not, have been consulted.

Occasionally, what started as a temporary country alliance became a permanent union.

Country Elevator
See ELEVATOR.

Country Giant
Country giants is one of the names given to country elevators.
See ELEVATOR.

Cowboy Coffee
According to tradition, coffee only deserves the title of cowboy coffee when it will float a horseshoe. It also helps if it is brewed in an old tin can over an open fire and has the coffee grounds still in it, to be left in the bottom of the cup like tea leaves.

Cow Chips
Cow chips are broken, dried MEADOW MUFFINS. This is the cow's version of buffalo chips. Apparently, in a pinch, these could be used for fuel in the same manner as buffalo chips, although they do not burn quite so well.

Cow Gate
See CATTLE GATE.

Cow Horse

A cow horse is not the result of some strange attempt to cross these two animals. A cow horse is a horse used to work with cattle and a good cow horse is a cowboy's best asset. It has to be quick and agile and intelligent enough to fully understand what is expected of it as goes about its work. The QUARTER HORSE is renowned as a cow horse.

Cow Juice

Milk, of course.

Cow Poke/Cowpoke

1. A cow poke is a large wooden Y, often a naturally forked branch of a tree, placed around a cow's neck and lashed in place. Cow pokes are placed on cows that have learned that, with determination, they can force their way through a barbed wire fence. The flat arms of the Y effectively prevent the cow from spreading the strands of wire with its body.
2. Cowpoke was also a name for a cowboy. Whether the cowboy, who also kept the cattle from getting away, took on the name to also become a cowpoke, or whether the device was named after the cowboy, is unclear.

Cowpuncher

As cowboys have to physically handle cattle, especially at branding time, it didn't take long for them to pick up this nickname. It is common to all ranching country in North America.

Coyote

The coyote, whether pronounced ki´ot, ki´ut, or ki´o tee, is the small wolf-like member of the dog family whose lonesome, mournful howl is associated with the openness of the West. Perhaps more than any other sound, the cry of the coyote is the sound that symbolizes the open prairie.

CPR Section

The original agreement with the CPR for the building of the railway was 25 million dollars and 25 million acres of land. (In the end, it cost much more.) The 25 million acres constituted about half the land that had been surveyed to that point. Therefore, the odd-numbered sections in each township within 24 miles of either side of the railway were given to the CPR and were simply referred to as CPR sections.

CPR Siding

During the construction of the CPR, sidings had to be placed in the single track every so many miles to allow trains to pass. These sidings were named for identification. As there could never be a town for every siding, names for the sidings that remained without towns were known as the CPR Sidings. You have, for example, the CPR Siding of Newton, or simply, Newton Siding. Most of the sidings have now gone and, where there is no double track, the sidings required to allow trains to pass are found only in actual towns. Occasionally, what started as a siding did become a town but retained the CPR Siding name, as with Alpen Siding, Alberta.

CPR Strawberries

CPR strawberries are, in a word, prunes. In the early days of the pioneers, during the construction of the railway and during the Depression, prunes were an inexpensive fruit that could be kept in all weather without special precautions. Consequently, our forebears ate more prunes than they care to remember and, to this day, prunes may be referred to throughout the West as CPR strawberries.

There is one old witticism that goes something to the effect that, "As the prunes have not arrived, strawberries will be used for tomorrow's 'Strawberry Festival.'"

Cream Cheque

The cream cheque was extra money that came to the farm family from the sale of cream from the family cows. This was frequently the farm wife's money, as was egg money, since it was generally accepted that it was her job to separate the milk and set aside the cream. As a rule, the cream can was set out for pickup by the dairy twice a week. The dairy picked up the cream and left an empty can containing the cream cheque for the previous pickup. The cheques were small, but they added a little to the money the farm wife could call her own. See also EGG MONEY.

Cream of the Crop

This expression, which now is widely used to mean the best of a group, originally meant the best milk-producing cow on a dairy farm. This was not the cow that just gave the most milk, but the cow that combined quantity with quality, as judged by the amount of cream in the milk.

Crick

Crick is a corruption of creek, which is a very small river. Technically, a creek is a small waterway that runs into the sea, so there are very few real creeks in western Canada! However, this does not stop us calling our small streams creeks or cricks.

Crinklins

Crinklins is a Western pronunciation of crackling, or pork fat that has been rendered until it is brittle. Many people consider crinklins to be a real treat.

Critter

Originally, a critter was a yearling cow or steer. Over time, the term has come to be applied to any animal and even, jokingly, to small children.

Crow

In western Canada, any reference to the Crow has absolutely nothing to do with the bird. The Crow refers to the Crow's Nest Pass freight rates. Altered in the late 1980s amid great controversy, the Crow's Nest Pass freight rates benefited Western farmers by subsidizing the cost of transportation of grain to the West. The federal government made up the difference between what was charged and the actual cost in the form of the Crow Benefit.

During the debate in the House of Commons on the bill that would alter the Crow, farmers presented petitions that were in the form of crows with the petitioners' signatures on the back.

The end of the Crow contributed to the abandonment of rail lines that, in turn, accelerated the closure of the country ELEVATOR.

Crow Bait

Anything without sufficient meat on its bones, be it beast or person, is crow bait. Originally, the term applied only to skinny, worn-out horses, but it did not take long for it to be applied to all skinny beings.

Crowhop

Crowhop is a derisive, contemptuous description of mild bucking. On the rodeo circuit, when a horse or bull is doing a pathetic job of bucking, it may be referred to as doing a crowhop.

Crow's Nest

The crow's nest was a common term for the cupola of the freight train CABOOSE, when freight trains had cabooses.

Crow Storm

Just as summer gives us one last taste of nice weather during INDIAN SUMMER, so winter can give us one last snowy blast when it should be spring. This last gasp of winter, which comes after the commonly accepted sign of spring, the arrival of the crows, is known as the crow storm.

On 19 May 1987, the Edmonton area suffered a severe crow storm with freezing temperatures and over four inches of snow, well after spring had initially arrived.

Crush My Soul on the End of a Fence Rail

This is perhaps the oldest expression recorded in this collection. Apparently, it was one of the favourite epithets of the Northwest voyageurs. It expressed their love of wide open spaces and dislike for fences but, given the arduous and dangerous life of the voyageurs, it is hard to believe that they did not have a few more earthy expressions as well.

Cut

The routine castration of farm animals is simply referred to as cutting. To cut, therefore, is to castrate. See PRAIRIE OYSTER.

Cut a Wide Swath

A swath is the width of crop cut at one pass with the swather. As the wider the swath the more noticeable the passage of the swather, to cut a wide swath is to really make your mark, or make your presence felt, in whatever it is that you are doing.

Cutter

A cutter is a small, one-horse sleigh of many and varied designs. The cutter was the main means of winter travel when horses provided the motive power. If the buckboard was the pickup truck of the West, the cutter was the car, if not the sports car.

As in

Duchess, Alberta;
Denzil, Saskatchewan;
Deerhorn, Manitoba

Dab a Loop

To dab a loop is to successfully throw your lariat so as to rope the animal intended, in the manner intended.

Dainties

In the prairie provinces, the fancy cookies and cakes served with tea or coffee to guests at parties, or just personally enjoyed, are called dainties. Those from other parts of the country report that they were unsure what was expected when they were first asked to provide dainties for the school tea.

Dally

Dally does not just mean to loiter and take your time, as in to dally on the way to school. It also means to wrap your lariat around the saddle horn to secure it. When watching the steer roping at the rodeo you will see the cowboy, after roping the steer, dally his lariat so that the horse may hold the rope taut while he dismounts to throw and tie the steer.

Damp

Damp is the description of grain that has a moisture content of 17 percent or more. Moisture content is important when delivering grain to the elevator as the range from dry to damp is very narrow and affects the value of the grain. Grain with a high moisture content is tough and does not store well, being prone to rot.

Dead Cinch

Anything that is an absolute certainty is a dead cinch. Coming from the Spanish word *cincha*, for girth, the cinch is the strap that holds a saddle or pack in place on a horse. As it is essential that it hold firmly, to cinch became to fasten securely or to make absolutely sure of something. Somehow, somewhere, the absolute assurance of death got added and something that is absolutely certain became a dead cinch. In some instances, the expression is taken one step further and becomes, in a strangely contradictory expression, a dead, immortal cinch.

Deadfall

While deadfall is well known as a term to describe a treed area that is full of fallen dead trees, or even a single naturally felled tree, it is less well known as a type of animal trap once commonly used in western Canada. A deadfall is a trap, usually constructed on site out of wood found in the area, which kills an animal by dropping a heavy log on its head or back when the baited trigger is touched. A deadfall trap is most effective for trapping medium-sized animals.

Dead Furrow

When ploughing a field with an old single bottom, or single ploughshare, one-way plough, the first furrow turned earth onto the surface of the land rather than into the hollow of a previous furrow, forming a ridge. Conversely, the last furrow would be empty, as no earth is thrown into it to fill the trench. This last, empty furrow was known as the dead furrow.

Diefenbaker Meat

It has been reported that at some time during the Diefenbaker years there was a distribution of canned meat such as Spork or Spam, the kind of meat usually referred to as mystery meat. This distribution was apparently made to institutions and needy families, so it may have been done by local government agencies and was probably not directly attributable to John Diefenbaker. But, somehow, his name got associated with this distribution. In places where this meat ended up, people may still refer to canned meat as Diefenbaker meat or Diefenbaker steak.

Diggins

A diggins was a homesteader's, and now a farmer's, own coal mine, gravel pit, or other excavation from which something of value could be taken. While a private gravel pit might well be of some value today, it is unlikely that a farmer would bother to dig for coal. It was, however, the fortunate, and rare, homesteader who discovered a small pocket of coal. If you do not have a personal source of gravel in your own diggins, you may be tempted to take what you need from Section 37. See SECTION 37 for an explanation.

Digout

Yes, the prairies dig out after a snowstorm, but so does everyone else, and that is not the meaning of this word. It is not heard much these days, but it is not so long ago that across a large section of southern Manitoba, and perhaps into Saskatchewan, what is usually called a dugout was referred to as a digout.

Dingle Dangle

Unfortunately, this interesting expression seems to have become part of history. It meant to go your own way without worry or concern, as in, "I'll just dingle dangle and leave it all to you."

Dink

By now everyone has heard of this term as a name for modern young couples, being an acronym for double income, no kids. However, long before anyone dreamed up that one, the word had meaning for the cowboy. A dink is a horse that, either by lack of natural ability or training, is totally ineffective as a working horse. It might be fine for a Sunday ride and it might look good in the pasture, but it was never going to earn its keep as a working horse on the range.

Dinkies

Dinkies was the name Winnipegers gave to the electric street cars that could be operated from either end. No turn around or loop was required at the end of the line. The driver just lowered the overhead electrical contacts at one end, raised them at what would become the rear of the car, and moved to controls at the other end.

Dinner

Once again, things change with time, but traditionally dinner on the prairies has been the noon meal, rather than the evening meal as would be expected in most other places. Strictly speaking, dinner should be the main meal of the day, whether eaten at noon or in the evening.
For urban residents and those in most other parts of the country, the main meal is in the evening and, therefore, the term dinner is always associated with supper. Perhaps the hard-working farm family needed a substantial meal both at noon and in the evening. What is of importance here is that if you are invited to Sunday dinner in the West, you better make sure you know at what time of day dinner is being served. See also Lunch.

Dip

It is common enough to call a low spot in the road or in the field a dip but, on the prairies, large dips can become geographical features of the landscape. A dip may be named (often after the farmer on whose land it is located), or simply called the dip. But in either case, it is not just an incidental low spot, it is a locally known location from which directions can be given in much the same way as they can from the Correction Line.

Dirty Thirties

No one with prairie roots, and surely few others, need an explanation of this term. It refers to the Depression and all that went with the drought, the lack of employment, and often the lack of hope associated with those years. But the term is not a figurative expression meaning bad or hard times. The Depression affected the entire continent and elsewhere was called the Hungry Thirties, or simply the Depression Years. On the prairies those years were literally dirty. Severe drought dried out the farmlands allowing winds to pick up and carry the soil. Everything was constantly covered with a layer of dirt that settled out of the air. During this time the prairies became known as the dust bowl. A BLACK BLIZZARD not only caused the loss of valuable topsoil, but deposited that soil far and wide over everything and everyone. It was, in a very real sense, the Dirty Thirties.

Dockage

Dockage is the penalty deducted, or docked, from the value of a farmer's load of grain to make up for the shrinkage that will occur when the grain is cleaned and the weed seeds, straw, and other things (such as grasshopper parts!) found in the grain are removed. Dockage is determined at the time of delivery from samples taken from various parts of the load. The samples are cleaned and the results weighed. The same percentage is then applied to the entire load.

Dockage is not necessarily all loss. After the grain has been cleaned, the screenings may be retained by the farmer or perhaps sold. The screenings may be mainly mustard seeds, wild barley, and the like, which can be added to cattle feed and are, therefore, of some value.

Doctoring

Doctoring does not mean to be in the business of being a doctor. It means to be in the act of visiting the doctor or a series of doctors. After all, if going to a shop is shopping why shouldn't going to a doctor be doctoring? So don't be surprised if, when you complain about your health, someone asks if you are doctoring rather than if you are seeing a doctor.

This expression has also been heard in northwest Ontario but, after all, they are more like Westerners than the rest of Ontario.

Dominion Lands Survey

The survey system used in western Canada must be explained because of the number of words in the daily vocabulary of western Canadians that originate with that survey. This is not intended to be a detailed account of the survey; it is merely an overall description that attempts to bring together all the familiar words that are defined under their respective individual listings.

The survey mapped out a pattern of six-mile square TOWNSHIPS across the prairie. The grid on which these townships are based is comprised of east-west BASE LINES and north-south meridians.

Two townships are laid out to the south and two to the north of each base line, requiring base lines to be drawn between every fourth township. The first base line is the Canada-US border, or forty-ninth parallel. From there they form a series of parallel lines every twenty-four miles, plus road allowances, north to the limit of the survey. Townships are numbered north from the forty-ninth parallel with the first township being number 1.

The north-south reference lines for the survey begin with the PRINCIPAL MERIDIAN (or WINNIPEG MERIDIAN) which was drawn north from the border at 97°27′28.41″ west longitude (about fifteen miles west of Emerson, Manitoba). The townships were then marked out and numbered in RANGES, twenty-four miles plus road allowances wide, east and west of the Principal Meridian. Further meridians, numbered second, third, on through the sixth, were drawn at 102′W and every four degrees thereafter to the Rockies, with the ranges numbered to the west from these meridians. These meridians follow their degree of longitude exactly with no adjustment for convergence.

As the north-south lines between the townships are true meridians, they converge northwards. This means that township divisions drawn north and south from one base line do not meet exactly those drawn from adjacent base lines. A line parallel to the base line, and midway between each one, is the CORRECTION LINE, where a slight jog occurs to correct for the converging lines of longitude.

A township is identified by the number of townships north of the border and the number of ranges east or west of the Principal Meridian or west of any other meridian.

Each township, being six miles by six miles, is divided into thirty-six numbered sections, each one-mile square. (For the numbering pattern see SECTION.) Each section is divided into four quarter sections, or quarters. See QUARTER.

Between each township and each section there is a ROAD ALLOWANCE (see also ROADLOUNCE) of one and one-half chains (ninety-nine feet) in the first stage of the survey and one chain (sixty-six feet) in the later stages. The narrower road allowances are now being widened at the expense of the sections of land. The initial survey, however, allowed for the road allowance so that each township is actually six miles plus road allowances square.

A prairie birth certificate, based on the quarter section on which the birth occurred, could read for example, SE ¼ 26-13-4 W2. To those familiar with the system, this identifies a location as precise as any street address. It is the southeast quarter of section 26, township 13 (thirteenth township north of the Canada-US border), range 4 west of the second meridian (fourth range of townships west of 102° west longitude). That would be a location close to Kipling, Saskatchewan.

Begun in 1871 (after initial attempts had been halted by the Métis, who feared for their land), the Dominion Lands Survey, when completed, covered more than 200 million acres of land in the three prairie provinces and a small portion of British Columbia.

It is difficult to imagine the enormity of the job and the precision with which it had to be done without the benefit of Global Positioning System satellites and other modern aids to surveying. However, with the entire land mass surveyed, and the road system based on miles and acres, it is easy to understand the resistance toward the change to the metric system of kilometres and hectares.

Don't Crack Your Crupper

The crupper, pronounced krup´er, is both the hindquarters of a horse and the part of a horse's harness that fits over the hind end and under the tail. When used now, the expression simply means don't bust your butt or other words to that effect. It can be either one of genuine concern or a sarcastic remark to a shovel leaner.

Doozer

If something is a doozer, or doozie, it means that whatever is being described is big, great, or extreme. It fits into almost any situation—it can be a doozer of a storm, you can have a doozer of a cold, or it can be a doozer of a harvest. The only thing bigger and better than a doozer is a real doozer.

While it has been claimed that this comes from an old English word for a hearty blow, it seems far more reasonable that the expression comes from the Ukrainian *duze* meaning very, as in *duze dobra,* or very good. Mid-European immigrants would have referred to that which was big or exceptional as duze, which was corrupted to the English doozer or doozie.

Dough-Gods

Throughout southern Alberta, and from there to other parts of the West, the dumplings on top of the stew have been known as dough-gods.

Dragged

When the long, gravel, prairie roads are gone over with the grader in an attempt to smooth them out, an effort which many would consider is usually unsuccessful, the road is dragged. While the road is being dragged or will be dragged and might have been dragged, the past tense often became the unique drugged, as in, "They drugged our road yesterday but it's as bad as ever!"

Dragging Money

In areas with a large Icelandic population, it is reported that people sometimes speak of dragging, or draggin', money out of the bank. While many people may feel that getting money out of banks, especially if it is farmers getting loans extended, comes close to dragging it out, that is not the origin of the expression. As the Icelandic word for draw is *draga,* in communities where both English and Icelandic are spoken, it appears that the withdrawing, or drawing, moved from the draga of one language to the dragging of another. Both words apparently come from the same ancient root, and now centuries later, reunite!

Draw

A draw is a deep ravine running down into a COULEE from the flat tableland above. Formed by runoff water running down into the coulee, it is usually the easiest route up out of the coulee to the upper countryside.

A draw may also be a valley, shallower than others around it, between rolling hills. The draw would not have a river or stream in it as other valleys might.

Canada's range country never experienced the same gunslinging, Wild West times that have become associated with the opening of the western United States, the verb draw, as in, to draw your six shooter, did not attain the same fame in western Canada as it did south of the border.

Draw Two

Draw two was a familiar cry in the men-only beer parlours of the past. For that matter, it may still be heard in hotel beer parlours today, although it is unlikely, since beer is now often sold by the pitcher. The cry could have been draw two, or four, or six, or any even number depending on the number of men at the table, as draft beer was always sold by twos, the legal limit you could have on the table, per person, at any time.

Interestingly, men must have gone to the pubs in groups of three, as most people when speaking of this expression first mention draw six. See also TWO AND A JUICE.

Duds

Bearing no known relationship with dud ammunition, or other ineffectual or unsatisfactory things, duds are your clothes. This definition is found in most dictionaries, but it seems to be far more prevalent on the prairies than elsewhere. In addition, elsewhere duds are often old work clothes, while in the West your Sunday best are still your duds—actually, Sunday best duds.

Duff's Ditch

The Winnipeg Floodway, properly called the Red River Floodway, is frequently referred to as Duff's Ditch. Named after Duff Roblin, premier of Manitoba at the time of its construction, the term was originally used by detractors of the project who claimed that it would never work and was therefore a waste of money. Those living immediately south of the control gates may still curse its existence at times, but those living within the city are now very grateful for Duff's Ditch, as it has carried flood waters around the city many times.

Built between 1962 and 1968, the floodway is a channel twenty-nine miles long and from thirty to sixty-five feet deep. Its construction required the removal of approximately one hundred million cubic yards of earth, more than was moved to create the St. Lawrence Seaway. At the time of construction, it was the world's largest earth-moving project since the construction of the Panama Canal. When in full operation, the floodway can carry Red River flood waters around the city at a rate of 60,000 cubic feet per second. Perhaps its biggest claim to fame is that it was a major government undertaking that was completed on time and under budget!

A recent proposal would increase the size of the floodway and divert much of the Red River into it year-round instead of just during flooding. The purpose would be to gain greater flood protection and a constant water level for Winnipeg, while also providing an excellent site for various water sports.

Dugout

1. The farm dugout, also known as a DIGOUT, is an artificially made hollow or pit to collect runoff water, thus creating a pond for a summer water supply. Prior to easy accessibility to well drilling, it provided water for the home as well as for the animals.

   The dugout is also the farm child's swimming hole on hot summer days. In this respect it has, unfortunately, been the scene of many prairie tragedies. Parents, miles from any other water, lived with the knowledge of the dugout's potential danger. There are few who did not, when a child repeatedly failed to answer a call, hear the chilling words, "Better check the dugout."

2. The term also applied to a temporary home carved into the prairie sod and covered with canvas or lumber. This served as a home while the cabin was being built. Later the dugout, especially if well roofed with wood and sod, became the food storage area, the closest thing to a cold room. Such storage rooms can still be found today and will still be called the dugout.

One interesting feature of the dugout house was that, when roofed with dirt, it was not unknown for the roof to be used as a garden for the growing of vegetables. A dirt-roofed dugout, however, was even more subject to indoor rain after a day or two of rain outside. See also SODDIE.

Dumb as a Post

How dumb can you be? Someone or something may be as dumb as a post and that is pretty dumb, but perhaps not as dumb as in the next expression.

Dumb as a Sack of Hammers

Now that is the height of a lack of intelligence!

As in

Easier to Jump Over Than to Go Around

This is one way prairie folk have for describing short, fat individuals or things.

Egg Money

Egg money was, and in some cases may still be, the money generated by the sale of eggs from chickens kept on the farm. These are not eggs sold commercially, but rather simply sold to neighbours or friends and relatives in town. Like the milk cheque, egg money is traditionally the property of the farm wife, who is probably the one who does most of the work around the hen house, including collecting the eggs. It is not a great amount of money, but it adds a little to that pot of money on the kitchen shelf that she can call her own, as distinct from the general farm income.

In the days when most wives did not work outside the home, many city women envied their farm counterparts, as the urban housewife had no source of money other than her husband. Even if she saved from the grocery money, when she bought her husband's birthday present she was really using his money. The farm wife, however, had her own money— egg money and the CREAM CHEQUE.

Elevator

The old grain elevators on the prairies are more properly called country elevators to distinguish them from terminal elevators. But the addition of the word country was not required across the prairies to identify these most recognizable of prairie structures. These prairie giants are the objects most commonly used to symbolize the prairies and prairie life. Spotted along the railways at regular intervals, these tall, uniquely shaped buildings were designed to take grain from the farm trucks, store it and then load it into railway grain cars. While in storage, the grain may be cleaned and/or dried depending on what equipment is available at that elevator.

Proudly displayed on the sides of every elevator, in bold letters, is the name of the company that owns the elevator, and, in smaller letters, the name of the town in which it is located. These facts are so obvious to prairie residents that they are beneath mention. However, the story is told of a young British airman during World War II who was learning to fly in Saskatchewan at one of the training centres scattered across the prairies. Helplessly lost above miles and miles of flat countryside with, for him, no distinguishing features, he radioed for help. Ground control, prairie born and raised, could not understand the problem and gave the obvious advice. Find a railway track, follow it to a town, read the town's name off the elevator, find that town on the map and head home. After lengthy radio silence, ground control called the pilot to ask what was happening. Sheepishly, the pilot replied that he was still lost. He had found and followed a railway track and had, by that time, flown over five towns called Searle, none of which he could find on the map.

For a number of reasons, the new, huge, concrete and steel regional elevators, called high through-put grain handling centres, are disliked by many people. The closure and eventual destruction of the old elevators may be associated with the abandonment of another rail line and contribute to the death of another small prairie town. It means that grain must be hauled much longer distances and that means utilizing much bigger trucks. Bigger trucks mean more expense for farmers and more damage to the highways.

The list of grievances goes on and on, but the end of the Crow rate and economy of scale have sealed the fate of the old prairie giants. In a very short time the only ones left will be the few that remain as museums. It is the sad passing of a prairie icon.

The name elevator comes from the lifting of the grain from where it is dumped to the top of the building, from where it can be dropped into the correct storage area or to a waiting grain car. See also CROW.

Empties Going East/Back

As a very general rule, the prairies ship in manufactured products from elsewhere and ship out grain and raw material. As these products travel in different railway cars, trains on the prairies often contain empty cars deadheading back for another load. They are simply referred to as empties going west, east or back.

From this derives another expression of empties going east or back, referring to clouds which, in time of drought, pass overhead without giving rain, having been emptied of the necessary moisture before reaching the prairies.

In her poem "The Wind Our Enemy," Anne Mariott wrote:

So soon the sickly-familiar saying grew,
(Watching the futile clouds sneak down the north)
"Just empties going back!"

Unfortunately, this expression may be heard again across much of the prairies if the weather patterns of the last couple of years do not change.

Engines

In a holdover from the old days on the farm when a steam engine drove the threshing machine many farmers still talk about their engines rather than their tractors.

Heavy equipment operators also speak of engines, whereas others might use the term motors. In doing so, they are making the distinction between an electric motor and an internal combustion engine.

Evener

The evener was part of the double-tree harness that evened the load between the horses, ensuring that both shared the work evenly. It was, in fact, the double-tree of a double-tree harness. The term eveners was used especially when there were three horses and the double-tree had to be off centred to ensure an even pull.

From this, any device, trick, or rule that divides anything evenly, from a workload to the after-dinner pie, may be an evener. The old trick of one cut and one pick first, to get two children to divide something evenly, is an evener.

As in

Finger, Manitoba;
Faust, Alberta; Fairy
Glen, Saskatchewan

Fall Supper

Fall supper is now a more common name for what was traditionally known as a FOWL SUPPER. It is an annual event across the prairies, usually taking place in October and often in conjunction with Thanksgiving. Featuring turkey or other fowl, the supper is put on by a church or other community group in order to raise money. Everyone in the group contributes to the preparation of the dinner and tickets are sold to the general public.

As it combines the rural attributes of good home-cooked food and good company, people travel many miles to take part in a fall supper. Radio stations in many cities across the prairies announce the location of fall suppers as a public service and vast numbers of city people drive out into the country for this yearly treat. It is also a time when those who have moved to the city return home to visit with their old friends and neighbours.

Farmer's Tan

While often the object of derision in the city, especially among the beautiful people who spend a great amount of time and money working on their tans, a farmer's tan is a badge of the occupation. It consists of heavily tanned lower arms and V at the neck, with a white torso, shoulders, and upper arms. It is the result of working long hours outdoors in a shirt with the sleeves rolled up and the top button at the neck undone. The deep tanning of the face by sun and wind ends midway up the forehead, the upper part remaining white where it has been protected by the TRACTOR CAP.

The white of the upper arms extends down almost to the elbows, as the farmer has traditionally worn a long-sleeved shirt with the sleeves rolled up, rather than a short-sleeved T-shirt. This may be changing somewhat today, but a long-sleeved shirt allows the sleeves to be rolled down when handling chemicals, when working in dusty conditions, or when the bugs and mosquitoes are bad.

Feeders

While some may claim that feeders are the spouse's relatives arriving at mealtime, they are actually cattle that are bought to be fattened for market.

Feeling his Oats

A person who is feeling his or her oats is rambunctious, full of energy, and raring to go. The expression comes from the belief, if not the fact, that a horse that has had a feed of oats instead of, or with, its regular hay gets an extra shot of energy and is, therefore, feeling its oats.

Ferstay

Here is another word borrowed from another language and brought phonetically into English. Ferstay, ferstai, furstay, or however else it may be spelled, is believed to be the English rendition of the German *verstebe*, meaning understand. In English, it is used in place of the word understand at the end of an explanation or set of directions, as in, "Do you understand?" Ferstay can also replace "Understood" or "I understand" as a response.

The only difference between the word when it is used as the question, "Do you understand?" and the statement, "I understand" is the rising inflection when it is used in the former case. Ferstay?

Few Pickles Short of a Jar

This is one prairie version of the few bricks short of a load expression, indicating someone who is not too swift mentally. The same deficiency may also be referred to as being ONE ROOSTER SHORT OF A BARNYARD.

Finishing the CPR

As noted under CPR SECTIONS, sections of land in every township went to the CPR to help cover the cost of building the railway. If this land was leased, the farmer working the lease referred to the land as the CPR so, if he was out finishing the CPR, it was clearly understood that he was finishing work on the leased CPR section. In exactly the same way he might be finishing the school or finishing the Bay but, as half the land in many townships belonged to the CPR, it was most often that land that was leased.

For some reason finishing is the most frequently mentioned term, but the farmer could also be starting or working the CPR.

Fireguard

The fireguard, or firebreak, is a ploughed or disked strip around an area to protect it from a prairie fire. Back when huge prairie fires were a very real danger, an adequate fireguard around the house and barn could literally be the difference between life and death. At the very least it was the difference between losing or saving your cabin and all your possessions.

There is a poignant painting by Sheldon Williams, entitled *The Fire Guard* (*Prairie Fire*), that shows a farmer amid the smoke from a prairie fire, desperately ploughing a fireguard with a single-bottom plough and frightened horses, and the farmer's wife beating at the flames with a sack. See also BURN.

Fishing

Fishing is a term used on the rodeo circuit when the rider has missed with the rope, or failed to DAB A LOOP but, either by accident or by flicking the rope, the miss turns into a legal catch. The cowboy actually failed but, by luck more than skill, made the catch by fishing.

Fives

See NICKEL LARGE.

Flag

See SHOW A FLAG.

Flake of Hay

A flake of hay is a small part of a bale, about a forkful. The term is sometimes used with other things, such as straw, but the most common association is with hay. Small children can be sent for a flake of hay as it is within their ability to carry.

Flapjacks

Surely everyone knows that pancakes should be called flapjacks. Between the Calgary Stampede and the Grey Cup parade (especially when the Stampeders are in the game), every Canadian must surely have heard of flapjacks.

Foot Burner

Foot burner is a term used to describe the old horse-drawn, single-bottom plough that the farmer had to walk behind and guide. Those who walked behind a plough all day, keeping their footing in the freshly turned furrow and keeping the plough straight, say that it is a more fitting term than the rest of us can imagine.

If you were using a twelve-inch plough, the size typical of many of those used to break virgin prairie sod, you would walk about 8¼ miles for every acre ploughed. It was not unheard of to break 100 acres in a season when there was no great problem with rocks, roots, or weather. To break that 100 acres meant walking about 825 miles behind the plough, almost the distance from Winnipeg to Edmonton by road, and to do so controlling the horse and the plough.

Fowl Supper

Fowl supper is the traditional name for what is now more commonly called a FALL SUPPER. Perhaps confusion between fowl and foul led to the change in name.

Freak

A freak is a saddle that is made with very wide, puffy sides with deep depressions into which a rider's legs fit. It is designed to help the rider stay in the saddle when the horse is bucking. A freak in no way resembles an ASSOCIATION SADDLE and, as the term suggests, would be the object of derision at any rodeo.

Freeze to it

Westerners will often say freeze to it or frozen to it instead of the more common stick to it, stick at it, or other such sticking expressions. This may be a reflection of the prairie winter, but is more likely an extension of the use of the term in curling. In curling, a rock is frozen to another when it is up against it in such a way that it cannot be moved, as hitting it will only move the rock behind it.

Freshening Pork

Fortunately, we no longer have to salt meat, such as pork, in order to keep it for any length of time. However, our forefathers did, and to remove some of the salt to make it more palatable was to freshen the pork. Freshening pork was done by repeatedly boiling the salted meat in fresh water. Each boiling removed a little more salt (and a little more flavour).

Speaking of salt curing, do you remember Habicure, the special salt for curing meat? The fact that there are still people who remember Habicure and salt-cured meat is a reminder of how fast change takes place.

Fresno

The fresno was the horse-drawn forerunner of the dragline. Looking much like the modern dragline, but pulled by six or eight horses, it was used extensively across the prairies to build the thousands of miles of dirt roads that crisscrossed the landscape. The fresno removed earth from the borrow pit and spread it on the site of the road construction.

Frog Skin

Being green, one-dollar bills were often called frog skins. The term
disappeared when the dollar bill was replaced with the one-dollar coin.

Frost Boil

A frost boil is a graphic description of the eruption in a road during
spring thaw that results in a hole in the road. During the repeated
freezing-thawing cycles in spring, moisture gets trapped in numerous
cracks and crevices in the road and between the roadbed and paved
surface. The tremendous force of freezing water buckles the pavement,
pushing it up like a boil coming to a head.

Once the frost boil has broken the surface, it leaves a POTHOLE.
The most heavily paved and reinforced roads can be torn apart in a few
days of spring weather.

Funny as a Banker

Anyone who has renegotiated a farm
loan knows that bankers are not noted
for their humour, even though they may
frequently be referred to as comedians!
There has not been a lot of laughter
heard in bank offices on the prairies
lately, unless it was hysterical.

While the expression may be, for
good reason, currently in use, it originated
during the Depression years of the 1930s.

Funny Money

The Alberta Social Credit party had some unique monetary ideas, among
which was its own scrip. This scrip was quickly dubbed funny money.

Bill Aberhart, best known as Bible Bill and founder of the Social
Credit Party of Alberta, won the 1935 election in Alberta with his
promise of a $25 monthly dividend to all Albertans. However, the
Supreme Court of Canada ruled this, and most of his funny money
policies, *ultra vires*.

As in

Goodfare, Alberta;
Galilee, Saskatchewan;
Gods Lake, Manitoba

Galician

Whether these eastern-European immigrants came from the area properly called Galicia or not, they were called Galicians. They provided much of the labour for projects such as the railway and stayed on to help form the backbone of the prairie population. After the railway construction, they were a main source of labour in the lumber camps in winter as they sought to augment what little they made from meagre farms in the summer. The general contempt for these people implied by the term, and the frequent exploitation by employers, is hard to understand in a land where most people were immigrants.

Gang Plough

A gang is a bunch of people, so a gang plough is a bunch of ploughs, or more properly, several ploughshares in one implement. Large gang ploughs became possible with the advent of tractors that had enough power to pull several ploughshares through the earth. Without a tractor it would have taken six horses to pull what would now be considered a small gang plough.

Gang Saw

As with the gang plough, the gang saw is a bunch of saws in one. Used in a sawmill, it can cut one piece of lumber into several boards at one pass.

Gate Manners

Gate manners (or gate etiquette) are very simple—leave gates as you find them. If you find it open, leave it open. If you find it closed, leave it closed. Nothing can be quite as infuriating as looking for stock that wandered off through a gate someone else left open. Or, for that matter, having a driven herd milling about because they can't get through a closed gate that you left open.

Gear

The term gear, other than when dealing with gear wheels, really means the equipment required to do a job. A cowboy's gear includes his saddle and lariat. Gradually this term has come to mean all of your possessions. To pack your gear means to pack all that you have, although it reflects a lifestyle where probably all that you own is related to your work.

Get Your Rear in the Saddle

This is the rangeland equivalent of get your rear in gear or other such expressions meaning to get going or get moving. As with all these expressions, rear can be replaced with any number of other terms as crude or polite as you wish.

Gigging

Gigging, pronounced to rhyme with rigging, is a method of ice fishing in which the fish is snared. In the crystal clear lakes of the Duck Mountain area of Manitoba, and perhaps elsewhere, fish are clearly visible to some depth in the water. When gigging, a hole is cut in the ice and two lines are lowered but kept in sight. One is a noose, usually made of light copper wire. The other is a bright lure to attract the fish. When a fish, moving slowly in the very cold water, comes to investigate the lure, the snare is gently passed over the tail end and pulled sharply up behind the gills.

Gimli Glider

The Gimli glider was the Air Canada aircraft that ran out of fuel on a flight from the East to Edmonton on 23 July 1983, and glided to a landing at the old air force base at Gimli, Manitoba.

Now, anyone who runs out of gas and sheepishly has to go looking for a gas station and a can of gas may be referred to as a Gimli glider or having pulled a Gimli glider.

Glomming

Glomming is an expression that simply means to be hanging around, killing time, doing nothing—just glomming about. It is from the Scots word *glaum*, meaning clutch or grab, but also sounds a lot like the word glomerate, meaning to cluster together. But those who used to glomm around don't seem to have heard of *glaum* or glomerate. On most Saturday nights, the boys in town gathered on the main street, just glomming around, to see who had come into town and what was going on. Or, perhaps you were glomming around to see what, or who, you could GLOMM ONTO.

Glomm onto

Coming from glomming around, to glomm onto is to grab hold of an opportunity when it presents itself, to grab hold of when you get the chance, or to grab hold and not let go. While glomming about on a Saturday night, a young man might just happen to meet someone special and glomm onto the chance to ask her out.

Go Back and Forth

To go back and forth is to visit back and forth as you do between friends. Over a large area of the prairies, if you wish to state that you are close friends with someone, you need only say that the two of you go back and forth.

The expression originated from the fact that your neighbours could (and still can) be miles away and your friends scattered over a very large area. Visiting a friend could be an all-day affair requiring an early start in the morning if you were to have any time together before heading home again. Often it might mean staying overnight to make the long trip worthwhile. The fact that you made the effort to go back and forth indicated a strong friendship.

Go Back Land

The go back land is your homeland. During the settlement of the West, everyone came from somewhere else. The land you would have gone back to, if you could have gone back, was your go back land.

The vast majority of immigrants did not really want to go back, and didn't have the time or the money if they had wanted to. But there was always an emotional tug and memories of your homeland, your go back land, where relatives lived that you knew you would never see again.

Go Between

Not the third person between two disputing sides but a version of the COW GATE. A go between is simply two posts set so close together that, while a person can go between them, cattle cannot. A go between removes the necessity for the second short fence of the cow gate.

Going to See the Prairie Bears

In days when we were not as uninhibited as we are now, we needed other ways to say that we were going to the bathroom. When the bathroom consisted of the outdoor BIFFY, the trip could be referred to as going to see the prairie bears. As, with the door left open, one had a good view of the fields while sitting on the biffy, it is probably a play on going to see the prairie bare.

There were many other expressions that meant that the person was headed to the biffy. Going to spend a penny or SEE A MAN ABOUT A HORSE/DOG are just a couple of them.

Goldeye

Manitoba takes pride in being the source of that international delicacy, goldeye. The goldeye that is served for dinner is actually the fish of that name, a fish found in Lake Winnipeg and its tributaries, which has been smoked and dyed. You may not be aware, however, that much of what sells as goldeye is actually mooneye, a fish even the experts have trouble distinguishing from the true goldeye.

Gomer Bull

A gomer bull is a bull that has undergone one of several operations to enable his sperm to be more easily collected for use in artificial insemination. The irony is that, although the operation prevents him from actually mating with the cows, in the end, he will impregnate more cows than he could ever dream of!

Goose Birds

The goose birds are the northern juncos, properly called Oregon juncos (*Junco oreganus*), that arrive back, every year, at the same time as the geese. While they do not travel with the geese, they arrive together often enough for the juncos to have become known as the goose birds.

Goose Month

Goose month is the month when the geese head north again and you hear the honking and see the great Vs, or skeins as they are properly called, in the sky. It is a sure sign that winter is over and farmers will soon be out on the land. Goose month is usually assumed to be April, although the geese may well be flying well into May as well.

Migratory birds crossing the West in the spring and in the fall are numbered in the millions, although this is greatly reduced from what it was years ago. Still, in spring and fall the sight of the great flocks of birds never ceases to be a source of interest. The most fascinating sight and sound of all is probably that of the geese honking their way across the sky.

Gopher

1. The Richardson's ground squirrel (*Spermophilus richardsonii*), that pesky little rodent of the prairies, is commonly called a gopher. Saskatchewan, which is a leader in the use of buried optic fiber cable, had problems ensuring that the steel wrapping used on the cable was sufficient to keep out the gophers. They will eat through just about

anything that invades their subsurface domain. The name gopher may, in fact, come from the maze of under-ground tunnels they create, as *gaufre* is French for honeycomb.

2. The use of the term gopher, as in "go for," to describe your helper or flunky, is so widespread that it can hardly be considered a prairie term. However, as the gopher is a prairie animal and as it is a play on words involving gopher, the expression may well have started in these parts. Until proven otherwise, we should take credit for it anyway.

Go Round

In a rodeo, a go round is one round of competition in which each contestant performs once. In a big rodeo there may be a go round each day with go round money for the daily winner. The final winner is the cowboy who has amassed the most points after all go rounds have been completed.

From this, a go round has become an expression meaning one chance or one opportunity. You may be told that you have only one go round, or that you will have a chance at the next go round, or that this is your last go round.

Goul

Once upon a time, not so long ago, and perhaps even today in a few places, a goul, which rhymes with cool, was the thing on the hockey rink into which you tried to shoot the puck—the thing some other people call a goal.

Goulie

If you talk about the goul in hockey, then the guy who stood in front of the goul was the goulie.

Government Beef/Meat

Government beef, or government meat, is meat obtained by legally hunting on government land. See also JUMPER STEAK and QUEEN'S MUTTON.

Government Jewellery

Government jewellery includes the old ball and chain, leg shackles, handcuffs, or whatever other restraints law enforcement officers may use from time to time. Wearing government jewellery means being in prison, even when not actually wearing restraints.

Grabbing the Apple

Grabbing the apple, or more likely grabbin' the apple, is to grab hold of the saddle horn when riding a bucking horse. Grabbin' the apple is one way in which a rider can PULL LEATHER and, when done in saddle-bronc riding, it is grounds for disqualification.

Grain

Grain is the generic term that applies to all cereal crops. A grain farmer may be growing any one, or all, of a variety of crops.

Grain Crusher

A grain crusher, described under CHOP, is the machine that turns grain into chop for cattle feed.

Grain Doors

When grain is loaded into an older boxcar, normal sliding doors will not work. The doorway must be closed from the bottom up to allow the car to be filled. These doors are called, strangely enough, grain doors. The modern, cylindrical, steel grain cars do not, of course, require grain doors.

Grain Scoop

A grain scoop is a shovel used for moving grain that differs from a normal shovel in that it is covered, or enclosed at the handle end. It looks like a pail, flattened on one side and attached to a handle.

Grain Shovel

A grain shovel is simply a large shovel for moving grain. Unlike the grain scoop, it does not have a covered area at the handle end. Grain shovels make excellent snow shovels as long as you have the strength to move that much snow in one scoop. However, compared to shovelling grain, shovelling snow is child's play.

Great White Combine

The prairie hailstorm, the kind that is so destructive to crops, is the great white combine. The term is especially applicable when the hail comes just as the crop is ready for harvest and the summer's work is lost to the great white combine. The term has also been applied to an early snowfall that destroys a crop, but it is the hailstorm that is the most frequent and feared great white combine. See also LODGED.

Grenree

The grenree, or granree, is the place you store grain. The word is really spelled granary, but is seldom pronounced that way.

Grid

The grid is the pattern of roads and road allowances across the prairies. Should you ever doubt the symmetrical grid pattern across the prairie landscape, take a good look at it from a plane. The grid involves the division of the landscape into square townships, each containing square sections.

Grid Road

1. A grid road is one that follows the division, or road allowance, between townships and between sections. While roads are not usually built between all sections, the grid road system frequently divided the

township into eighteen rectangles rather than thirty-six squares, as would be the case if all road allowances were used.

2. In Saskatchewan, a grid road is particularly one that was built during the Grid Road Program, a program commenced in the 1950s to build roads on the grid patterns.

Grid roads are normally built by the province, but maintained by the municipality.

Grinners

It is the fortunate farmer who has not spent time picking rocks, western Canada's legacy from the glacial age. Most farmers have names for rocks that are largely unprintable, but grinners is one of the more imaginative terms for those rocks that are just showing through the surface of the ground. These are just sitting there with their little circular edge grinning at you. They form the first of the terrible trio—grinners, sleepers, and strollers. See SLEEPERS and STROLLERS, as well as INTERLAKE POTATOES.

Grommets

Grommets is one of several terms heard with reference to small children. It is not an unkind term; in fact it is used rather affectionately, as in, "Just keep the little grommets out of my way until I have finished my work." As the real grommet with which a Westerner would be most familiar is the metal eyelet, heaven only knows how the term came to apply to children.

Growlies

If you have had your growlies you have been fed. As this term refers to the prevention and curing of stomach growls, rather than to the cause of them, it can apply to all food, be it good or bad, fancy or plain.

Grubbing

Grubbing is the act of cutting trees, pulling stumps, and clearing bush in order to open up land for farming or other use. Grubbing, prior to the arrival of the cat, was backbreaking labour.

Grub Hook

1. A grub hook was a device used to help pull roots when grubbing.
2. Grub hooks are also your hands, as in, "Keep your grub hooks off my sandwich." In this case, the reference is not to grubbing land but to food, your grub hooks being the things with which you grab your grub.

Gumbo

Gumbo is the heavy clay soil prevalent in many area of the prairies that, when wet, becomes very sticky and clings to everything. When you walk in gumbo your feet get bigger and bigger until you can hardly lift them and you have to stop and carve off some of the mud.

Gumbo is one of those things in which people take a perverse pride, everyone claiming that their area has the worst (or is it the best?) gumbo. Despite the claims of others, Red River gumbo has achieved fame as the gumbo against which all other gumbos are measured.

Western Canada is famous for the width of the main streets in many of its cities and towns. This did not come about because our forefathers, with great foresight, predicted the need for multi-lane roadways to handle our present day traffic. It was simply the need to provide enough room for wagons to stay out of each other's ruts when it was wet and the gumbo was at its worst.

Gum-Rubber Boots

Rubber boots, so necessary in the gumbo, are frequently called gumboots or gum-rubber boots. Rubber boots must be just about universal and gumboots is very European. The two together provide a distinctly Western, and often ethnic, expression.

Gut Bombs

Can you think of a better term for hamburgers served at fairgrounds or exhibition grounds? The rodeo riders who follow the circuit living off the fare of amusement ground food booths are credited with this expression. Sometimes the suspicion is that the tough old Brahma bull that disappeared off the circuit after one too many CROWHOPS has ended up giving the cowboys new pain in the form of the many gut bombs they ate.

Gut Wagon

1. Growing out of what it can do to your insides on a rough prairie road, a gut wagon is your beat up old half-ton.
2. A gut wagon is also the wagon, or truck, that hauls the entrails and other waste away from the abattoir. Many will remember an old expression about an ugly face being one that could knock a dog off a gut wagon.

As in

Hearts Hill, Saskatchewan; Hadashville, Manitoba; Hondo, Alberta

Half-Mile Lines

As a section of land is one-mile square, the lines dividing the section into quarter sections are called either half-mile lines or QUARTER LINES.

Harness Rack

An old or otherwise decrepit horse, no longer any good for work, is nothing but a harness rack. See also CROW BAIT.

Harvest Excursion

The harvest excursion was a train that brought the thousands of labourers west to work the harvest in the fall at a time when the process was far more labour-intensive than it is today. Of course the term was facetious. It could not be considered an excursion in the usual sense of the word as work on the threshing crews was anything but a holiday.

Today, it is the market gardens that require intensive labour for their harvest. While there are no harvest excursions to bring in their labour, there may be a controversial importation of work crews from outside the country.

Harvestore

A trade name that has come into the language for the object associated with it, a Harvestore is the large, tall, cylindrical storage bin frequently seen on farms as one of the buildings on the HOME QUARTER.

Hay Burners

Hay burners are horses, as opposed to the coal and wood burners of the steam age, or the gas and diesel burners of today.

Hayloft

While not unique to the prairies, the hayloft is the upper storage area of the barn where hay is stored. Elsewhere, it is frequently called a haymow, but this term is seldom, if ever, heard on the farms of western Canada.

While the functional purpose of the hayloft was to store hay that could be thrown down to animals in the barn, it served a much wider purpose. It was a hiding place, a playground and, at times, a place for amorous liaisons.

Hay Lottery

Among all these terms from the past is one from the present. In 2002, farmers in eastern Canada donated hay to help those in the West affected by severe drought conditions. To achieve fair distribution of the hay, lotteries were held with eligible farmers and ranchers submitting their names for each draw. The odds of winning were small, with thousands of farmers hoping to win a portion of the limited amount of hay. Those that did win received one semi-trailer load of hay, approximately 15 tonnes. That is not a lot of hay, but it was greatly appreciated by those who received it.

Haymaker

Not a haymaker as in the roundhouse punch, but rather the great haymaker in the sky, the sun—sunshine being so essential to all ripening, including hay.

Hay Needles

Hay needles are sharp spears found in prairie grass. Hay needles can make a romp in the hayloft or haystack less comfortable than legend would have it, as many amorous young couples have discovered.

Hayseed

Hayseed is the familiar term for a country boy who is supposedly naive and unsophisticated. The word conjures up the stereotypical picture of the farm boy in bib overalls and straw hat with a piece of straw between his teeth.

Hayshaker

A hay shaker is a farmer. It is another of those terms that can be derogatory or not, depending on who is using it. Come to think of it, most terms for farmers can be somewhat derogatory depending on the situation and/or the person speaking.

Haywire

1. Haywire is the actual wire used to tie bales of hay and just about anything coming apart that needs to be tied together again.
2. Haywire also refers to something that is falling apart, confused, disorganized, or generally gone awry, as in, "This haywire outfit!" This usage comes, in part, from the horrendous tangle that can happen when a spool of haywire is mishandled, and sometimes even when it is property handled. It is akin to the tangle of fishing line on a reel, except that it is wire.

   It has been suggested that OUTFIT is the most useful word in a Westerner's vocabulary. This may be true but, if it is, haywire runs a close second.

Haze

To gather and drive livestock, especially from horseback, is to haze the cattle.

Header Barge

The header is the part of the threshing machine that cuts the head from the stalk. The header barge is an enclosed rack, lower on one side, that follows the header to catch the heads of grain.

Headland

For sailors, or those who live on the coast, a headland is a promontory sticking out into the sea. For the prairie farmer, a headland is the strip of grass at the end of the furrows in a fenced, cultivated field. It is not so necessary in this age of motorized equipment, but in the past it provided an area in which to turn the horses without them being on the ploughed surface.

Hectare

A hectare is that metric measurement of area that does not fit any original landholding in western Canada. It is 10,000 square metres, 2.471 acres, or one TRUDEAU ACRE, whichever you prefer. For easy comparison, a hectare is generally considered to be 2½ acres.

Heifer

A heifer is a young cow that has not yet calved, in other words, a virgin cow.

Heifer Dust

Heifer dust refers to an exaggeration or untruth. It is, of course, simply a more polite way of saying bullshit. After all, dust is a more acceptable word than shit and a heifer is a young cow as opposed to a crude bull.

Hell Bent for Leather

Hell bent for leather is a Western variation on the original expression hell bent for election. A rider on horseback pushing the horse as fast as it can go or a team at full gallop are going hell bent for leather. It conjures up a picture of the rider leaning far forward and a horse at full gallop with mane and tail flying or a team racing frantically on the verge of being out of control. Hell bent accentuates the danger of the speed to both horses and rider or driver.

This, and a number of other hell-bent-for expressions now refer to anyone in a mad dash or going about something as fast as they can, often without any obvious purpose.

Hen Fruit
What else would hen fruit be but another name for CACKLEBERRIES?

Herd Laws
In the early West, cattle were entitled to roam freely on open rangeland.
With ownership proved by the brand, fences were not only unknown but
were objects of derision. A fence was an Eastern abomination not in
keeping with the openness of the West. If you did not want cattle on
your land, then you would have to fence them out. Any laws that turned
that around and made the owner of livestock responsible for fencing in
animals are known as herd laws. While herd laws were a contentious
issue with cattlemen of the day, passage of these laws was a sign of
increasing settlement.

The poster advertising the 1908 Dominion Exhibition (Calgary
Stampede) showed a picture of a cowboy, with open plains behind him,
pulling up to a barbwire fence that crosses his path. There is a stook of
wheat on the near side. The caption reads, "Another trail cut off."

Hewsting
Parts of southern Alberta report that there is a tendency to corrupt
the political campaign term husting into hewsting. Therefore a politician
is out on the hewstings getting ready for the next election.
See also STUMPING.

Hightail
Coming from the trait of deer to lift their tails as they turn to run, this
well-known term, to hightail or to hightail it, simply means to get away
quickly. See also SHOW A FLAG.

Hobbled
A hobbled horse is one with a short strap, or hobble, tying its front legs
together so that its freedom of movement is severely reduced. This term
has expanded to refer to the restriction of a person's movement or
behaviour. This is a Western variation of the more common ball and
chain expression, in which marriage and a spouse become the hobble.

Hockey Pucks

These are not real NHL-approved hockey pucks; they are the frozen horse droppings, or ROAD APPLES, that so many of us played hockey with once upon a time. The usage was so common that it simply became the name for frozen horse manure. A good many boys who went on to become professional hockey stars scored their first goal with frozen horse manure, while wearing magazines stuffed in their socks for shin pads.

On the way to the rink it was routine to pick up several suitable pucks, as they did break up during a game and required replacement. (One set of local rules proclaimed that, if the puck broke when shot on net, the biggest part had to get into the net for it to count as a goal.) It was essential, however, that you remembered to remove unused spare pucks from your pockets before you went home and hung your coat up beside the kitchen stove.

It was also essential to clean pieces of broken pucks off the ice as, being a dark colour, they absorbed the sun and melted into the ice, making for a less than perfect skating surface. In those days you cleaned more than ice shavings off your skate blades!

While you would have trouble these days finding a hockey game being played with horse manure, many people still refer to frozen horse droppings as hockey pucks, or HORSE PUCKIES.

Home Quarter

The home quarter is the quarter section on which the farm buildings are located. See QUARTER.

Homestead

Generally speaking, a homestead is a piece of farmland on which a farmer is working and living. Strictly speaking, as a noun, a homestead was farmland granted under the terms of the Homestead Act of 1872.

As a verb, to homestead was to open land and start farming it, especially on land claimed under the terms of the Homestead Act.

The Homestead Act granted the head of a family, or any male over eighteen years of age, a quarter section (160 acres), of available Dominion land on the prairies. Available land did not include CPR, school, and Bay sections. When certain obligations were met, the person gained title to the land and earned the right to buy the adjacent quarter section at the going price, usually $2 to $3 an acre. For the obligations of the homesteader see PROVE UP.

Homesteader's Bible

The homesteader's bible was not the big family Bible that had been carried carefully all the way from the GO BACK LAND to this new home; it was the mail-order catalogue. For many years the T. Eaton Co. catalogue was the prairie homesteader's bible.

Mail-order catalogues are also known as wish books, a term reported to be commonly used by the Indians and Métis.

Homesteader's Fiddle

The homesteader's fiddle is the old two-handled crosscut saw. The expression comes not from trying to play it, as some people play music on a saw, but rather from the constant, rhythmical sound of the saw as land was cleared and logs cut for the building of a cabin. Today, the music of the homesteader's fiddle has been replaced by the far less appealing sound of the chain saw.

Honda

This honda is not the one you drive to work each day, but rather the eye in the end of a rope through which the rope is passed in order to make the running loop of the lariat.

Honkers

Honkers is the prairie farmer's and hunter's term for geese, especially Canada geese. Should anyone not understand this, they should stand outside anywhere in western Canada during GOOSE MONTH and listen as thousands of geese pass overhead.

Hoodoo

A hoodoo is the tall column of earth or stone that is left when the surrounding area of softer clay and shale has eroded away. The column, preserved by a cap of limestone or other hard rock, is frequently carved into a fantastic shape by the same erosion that created it.

Hoodoos are a striking feature of the landscape in the southern Alberta BADLANDS.

Hooey

1. In calf roping, when the cowboy ties the feet of the thrown calf, the half hitch with which the feet are tied is called a hooey. The string used to tie the hooey is a PIGGIN' STRING.
2. Hooey is also another term for ROAD APPLES or HOCKEY PUCKS, as in, "You're full of hooey."

'Hoppers

1. Grasshoppers in the West are seldom called grasshoppers; they are simply 'hoppers.
2. As a hopper can also be a container that holds something temporarily before being fed into something else, the large terminal elevators are sometimes facetiously called hoppers.

Horsed Off

Land that is horsed off has been grazed down by horses to the point that it is no good for the grazing of cattle until it is given time to recover. Horses do not graze as closely to the ground as sheep, but they tear the grass off closer to the ground than cattle. Therefore, horses can graze on land the cattle have been over, but cattle cannot graze on horsed-off land.

Horse Manure

Of course there is real horse manure, but as an expression horse manure is just another, more polite, variation of HEIFER DUST, which in turn is a variation of, oh well, you get the picture!

Horse Puckies

HORSE PUCKIES is another name for frozen ROAD APPLES coming from their use, once upon a time, as HOCKEY PUCKS.

House of Commons

While the House of Commons is that place down East where we send people to supposedly run the country, the house of commons (or the PARLIAMENT BUILDINGS), was a very common name, right across western Canada, for the BIFFY. Now that should tell you something about the way Westerners feel about the goings-on in Ottawa.

Hudson Bay Scot

See IMPROVED SCOTSMAN.

Hudson Bay Section

See BAY SECTION.

Hungry as 'Hoppers

If you have ever witnessed the damage done by an infestation of grasshoppers in a single day, then you need no explanation for this expression. The ravenous appetite of these creatures is legendary in many parts of the world and, despite the use of chemical defences, is still well known on the prairies.

The only thing to slow down a grasshopper infestation is a lack of food. "A 'hopper couldn't cross my place without a lunch pail," is an old joke from the Dirty Thirties.

Hunter

A hunter is the rodeo bull that tends to look for, or hunt, a thrown rider in order to go after him. When a hunter has thrown his rider, it is time for the rodeo clowns to earn their keep as it is their job to distract the bull from the fallen cowboy. The term may also be applied to other animals, especially horses, which tend to attack a thrown rider. From there the term may be used to describe a person, especially a business-person, who moves in for the kill when another business or business-person is most vulnerable.

Hurricane Deck

For a sailor the hurricane deck is a facetious name for an upper deck that is open to the wind, especially when used by passengers as the best place to view passing scenery. From there it has come to be the open, extremely windy front deck or open cockpit of a fast powerboat. But to the cowboy, especially the rodeo rider, it is the saddle of a wildly bucking bronc.

As in

Inwood, Manitoba;
Irma, Alberta;
Insinger, Saskatchewan

Icelandic Air Force

Around Gimli, Manitoba, with its large Icelandic population, the Icelandic air force refers to the large pelican population. The term probably came into existence when there was a large Royal Canadian Air Force training base at Gimli. The runways of that training base still exist and provided a landing strip for the GIMLI GLIDER.

Improved Englishman

Englishmen, especially the very English Englishmen, have not always been appreciated in the West. They tended to have a superior attitude, built on the days of the Empire, and to regard this new land as just another colony. It was not uncommon to see signs that read, "Help Wanted—Englishmen need not apply," especially in the Calgary area. (Obviously there were no human rights commissions in those days!)

An improved Englishman is, or at least was, one who has been in this country long enough to have lost some of his accent and have had some of his arrogance knocked out of him. He is not, however, to be confused with an IMPROVED SCOTSMAN. See also JELLY BAG ENGLISHMAN.

Improved Scotsman

Many of the early traders were Scottish and, therefore, many of the first Métis had Scottish fathers. A Métis of Scottish and Indian parentage was frequently referred to as an improved Scotsman. Another name for a

Métis with Scottish blood, considerably kinder to the Scottish father, was Hudson Bay Scot.

Indian Gift/Indian Giving

While this is no longer considered a politically correct term, its history provides an interesting example of cultural differences between Indians and prairie settlers. The Indians of western Canada lived a close-knit communal life. Ownership of possessions, as the whites knew it, was an unknown concept. One person might have possession of a certain item, but if another needed it he was perfectly entitled to help himself, whether or not the owner was around. This was a way of life that existed in the early days of settlement when, especially in an emergency, possessions could be borrowed freely. But the settlers were not prepared to accept the full concept of community ownership as practised by the aboriginal community. Therefore, the giving of a gift that could then be taken or borrowed back became known as an Indian gift or Indian giving.

However, whenever survival is at stake, it is generally accepted that if you need it you use it. While this seldom occurs in southern areas anymore, it is still a way of life in the North. It was certainly a way of life during the settlement of the prairies. If you needed shelter or food and came across a cabin, you made yourself at home. You never used all of the provisions and you replaced things that you could, such as firewood, before you left.

On the hill overlooking the town of Peace River, Alberta, is the grave of one famous pioneer, Twelve Foot Davis. The inscription on the gravestone tells us that he "never locked his cabin door." While the intent is appreciated, it draws smiles from those who understand the early West. They will tell you that the inscription had to be written by someone who really did not fully understand their history as, the truth be known, in the days of Twelve Foot Davis nobody would have dreamed of locking the cabin door.

Indian Squab

Indian squab is the common crow. It may be possible that Indians ate crow at times, either by choice or by necessity, but the thought was repugnant to most Europeans who facetiously named cooked crow after a European delicacy. Ironically, there are a lot of people who would view the eating of squab, or young pigeon, in the same way that they would see the eating of crow.

Indian Summer

While the term is widespread in North America, no one enjoys Indian summer more than those who live on the prairies. As the term refers to the period of warm weather that often follows the first taste of winter, prairie dwellers thoroughly enjoy these balmy days as they know only too well what is coming for the next several months.

Indian Wrestling

Indian wrestling is leg wrestling where the two opponents lie side by side and head to foot. They each raise the inner leg, locking it around the opponent's. The winner is the one who can roll the opponent over backwards. By its name it is assumed that this is a sport taught to the immigrants by the original inhabitants of the prairies.

Indian wrestling should only be conducted in a large area as the loser's arms and legs can flail around with considerable force. Many families tell tales of Uncle Charlie or Cousin Bob putting a hole in the wall or breaking a window at the height of an Indian wrestling competition.

Interdict List

The Interdict List was the list of those persons who had been barred from consuming liquor by the courts, usually for drunkenness or other drink-related offences. In those days, when permits were needed to purchase liquor and when public drinking places consisted of men-only beer parlours, it was possible to police such a list.

Interlake Potatoes

The Interlake area of Manitoba was left strewn with rocks by the retreating glaciers of long ago. Rock picking is a way of life and people speak of their rock farms. The rocks seem to grow in the ground year after year and you can't dig or plough without turning them up. Just when you think you are winning the battle, more appear. This vision of rocks growing in the soil year after year is reflected in the local reference to them as Interlake potatoes.

The feeling that these rocks had to be growing in the ground was so pervasive that there was a time when it was possible to find people who actually believed that rocks grew in size with pebbles becoming stones, which became small rocks, which, if left long enough, would become bigger rocks. While such an idea seems silly now, it was not so absurd to an unschooled settler who could find no other explanation for the fact that, a year after all the rocks thought big enough to be of concern were picked up, the plough was again turning up potato-sized rocks. See also PRAIRIE APPLES and PICKING ROCKS.

As in

Josephburg, Alberta;
Jordan River,
Saskatchewan;
Justice, Manitoba

Jack

Jack, or jackfish, is the Western term for the northern pike, or, if you are fussy, the *Esox lucius.*

Jag

No, jag is not an acronym for Judge Advocate General or the television show of that name. A jag can be one of two things.
1. A jag is a small load, especially a small load of wood or straw. For straw, it seems the size of a jag varies with the situation. If you are personally carrying it, a jag can be somewhere between a flake and a bale. If you are bringing it home in the truck, it is somewhere between a small bale and a full load. See also FLAKE OF HAY and BALE.
2. As being drunk is often referred to as being loaded, or having a load on, and as a jag is a small load, being just a little drunk becomes having a jag on.

Jam Pail Curling

All areas of Canada now produce excellent curling teams, but it is the prairie provinces that have traditionally been the centre of interest and activity for this sport. One form, seldom seen today, is for children to pour cement into old jam pails and use them as curling stones on river ice, flooded backyards, or just the naturally icy roads. What jam pail curling lacks in finesse, it makes up for in enthusiasm and fun.

Jelly Bag Englishman

The dislike of many Englishmen, noted under IMPROVED ENGLISHMAN, led to this term, which pulls no punches. The type of Englishman who looked down his nose at the strange beings in the colonies was considered to be worth no more than the contents of the jelly bag after the jelly had been made.

Jerk

This is the horse era version of a tow. To get a jerk, or a jerk home, was to use someone else's horses to get your wagon home.

The term may still be heard in rural areas, now meaning to get your truck or car, which has just died on the highway, towed home by a neighbour.

Jerk Fitting

A jerk fitting is a grease nipple on the farm equipment. It relates to the removal of the grease gun from that nipple.

Jerky

Jerky is dried strips of meat. Drying meat was a simple means of preserving it. Jerky could be carried for long periods of time, and, when reaching your destination took a lot of time, you could pass that time trying to chew it. The original jerky was a lot tougher than the item of that name sold in the corner store today. See also PEMMICAN.

Jigged/Jiggered

To be jigged is to be jostled, jerked around, or shaken up. While it originally meant to be physically jostled or shaken, it can also mean to be surprised or emotionally shaken as in, "Well, I'll be jigged!" This expression has now become, for some people, jiggered. But today it is probably only known by our grandparents.

Jigger

Quite apart from a device to measure liquor, a jigger may be one of two things.

1. A jigger is a simple but ingenious device that was developed by fishermen on Lake Winnipeg. In order to set a gill net under the ice, a jigger is used to run a line under the ice between two holes. It is simply a board with a sharp, hinged spike sticking up through a slot. The board floats up against the underside of the ice. A light line attached to the hinged spike is repeatedly jerked, causing the spike to propel the board along the underside of the ice to the next hole. As it goes it drags behind it the line that will be used to set the net.

2. A jigger is also that little hand-pumped, and later gas-powered, railway car used by section workers. This term is common to far more than western Canada but, with the long distances to cover on the prairie tracks, no one was more familiar with the sight of these efficient little carts than western Canadians. At the sight of the first gas-driven jiggers, many people wondered what the world was coming to, as it was a sure sign of just how lazy people were becoming.

Jitney

A jitney was a nickel, so all those things that once only cost a nickel incorporated the word. Cabs that cost a nickel per ride were jitney cabs and when streetcar fares were a nickel they were frequently called jitney cars.

Whether it was a nickel or more, a dance where a fee was charged for each dance and dance partner was a jitney dance. There appear to have been two types of jitney dances. One was the commercial dancehall where girls earned a living in remote towns populated mainly by men. The other was a means of raising money for community purposes.

Jumper

1. A jumper, or simply a jump, was a small single-seater sleigh that was often homemade.

2. A jumper is also a common term for either a deer or a rabbit. You can judge which one is being referred to by the context of the conversation, the location, the time of year, or the type of gun being carried.

Jumper Steak

As jumper is either deer or rabbit, it makes sense that jumper steak is either venison or rabbit meat. Being free meat taken from the great outdoors, most probably from government land, jumper steak was also called GOVERNMENT BEEF/MEAT.

As in

Kandahar, Saskatchewan; Klefeld, Manitoba; Kotscoty, Alberta

Keg

Keg is simply a contraction of muskeg; that is, when it is not a squat thing with beer in it.

Kicker

In the West, and especially in the northern areas of the West, a kicker is an outboard motor. The term refers mainly to a small outboard used either on a small boat or a larger boat when fishing. It is not a reference to one of those gigantic outboards with twice the power of the family car.

Kicks

Your kicks are, not surprisingly, your shoes. This term seems to surface in various areas throughout the West and goes nicely with nicks, or knickerbockers, to make your nicks and kicks. Strictly speaking, your nicks and kicks would be your pants and shoes, but it became an expression to mean all your clothing, as when you were wearing your Sunday best nicks and kicks.

Kinnikinik

Spelled this way or in several other ways, kinnikinik, pronounced kin nik´ in ik´, was a form of tobacco made from dry leaves and bark mixed with real tobacco. It was simply a way to make a small amount of tobacco go a long way, much to the detriment of the tobacco.

The word comes from various Indian languages and means that which is mixed together. It is too bad that the term is seldom heard these days as smokers, trying to observe new non-smoking rules, could try to kick kinnikinik!

Knee-High to a Grasshopper

Small things, especially small children, have always been referred to as knee-high to a grasshopper. Countless children have gritted their teeth while being told for the umpteenth time, with a pat on the head, "Why, the last time I saw you, you were only knee-high to a grasshopper!"

As in

**Ladywood, Manitoba;
Lobstick, Alberta;
Limerick,
Saskatchewan**

Lady Jane
Around Regina at least, this term is reported to be a reference to your common-law wife or girlfriend. This may not be part of permanent street language, but it is reported to be currently in the vocabulary of the area.

Land Office Business
With the passing of the Homestead Act, which made every head of a household and each male aged eighteen or over eligible to claim a quarter section of available Dominion land, men stormed the Dominion Land Offices. It was the sale crowd to end all sale crowds. To this day, any enterprise that is doing exceptionally well, with people beating a path to its door, is said to be doing a land office business.

Lease
A lease is land that is not owned, but has been leased for pasture, haying, or other such use. Land available to be leased may be Crown land or land owned by someone who does not wish to farm it. In the past, it could have been part of a CPR, school, or Bay section. Such land is simply referred to by the person working it as the lease.

Leg

A leg is the shaft running from the pit to the top of an ELEVATOR. In this shaft is the actual elevating apparatus, a moving belt with containers on it that carries the grain to the top of the building. From there it is directed into a chute that will drop it into one of the storage areas or into a waiting grain car.

Like a Chicken With Its Head Cut Off

Yes, a chicken can thrash around, by reflex action, after you have removed its head with an axe. If you have seen it, you know it is a good description of the extreme flap some people will get into now and then. This expression is claimed as a Western one only because more chickens have lost their heads on a chopping block on the prairies than elsewhere in the country.

Like Green Corn Through the Hired Girl

This is a variation of the many similes for as fast as, or goes through you like, that exist throughout the country. It is a saying suggesting great speed. It is an expression heard by many, especially if they hail from the vicinity of Poplar Point, Manitoba.

Lodged

Grain that has been flattened by the wind, rain, hail, or snow has been lodged. Sometimes a crop will be driven down to the point that it can only be cut by running the swather in the opposite direction to which the crop is lying. However, a truly lodged crop is down too far to be cut and is down permanently as the stalks have been broken, preventing any recovery.

Log Dog

See CANT HOOK.

Lonely as a Liberal

Over the years, Liberal MPs, and MLAs for that matter, have been few and far between on the prairies, even when their party was consistently in power in Ottawa. Amid the jokes about party conventions held in phone booths, emerged the expression lonely as a Liberal.

Longitudinal Centre of Canada

See CENTRAL CANADA.

Looking Up a Dead Horse's Ass

This is another of those expressions that sounds coarse, if not vulgar, but which actually has a sound basis in everyday living. During the days of true horsepower on the farm, the farmer had to be as much a veterinarian as farmer. When diagnosing ailments, one of the places that had to be examined, like it or not, was the animal's rectum. However, once your horse has died it is futile to be examining its rear end. Therefore, looking up a dead horse's ass has come into the language as the ultimate in futility. It can be heard in many forms including why look, as useless as looking, don't look, and like looking.

Loon Shit

This, believe it or not, is the only known name for a type of land surface common in areas of the prairies and northwestern Ontario. (Once again,

we will admit northwestern Ontario into the brotherhood of the West, whether they want it or not.) Loon shit is extremely marshy land composed of dead vegetation and its fair share of loon droppings. It is so wet that it undulates as you walk on it. You can walk carefully on the surface but, should you break through, you are up to your waist, or worse, in water. Engineers building highways in the Canadian Shield area of eastern Manitoba and northwestern Ontario complain of having to work with the two extremes, bedrock and loon shit, with nothing in between.

In some lakes in the area there are floating islands, complete with small trees, which are composed of loon shit. It is amazing to watch these drifting treed islands, on which it is possible to stand if you are careful, undulate in the wake of a passing boat, the trees bobbing and swaying with the wave action.

Loper

The loper is the grey wolf of the plains. The term is from the French *loup*, the word for wolf, but also brings to mind the long loping strides a wolf takes as it runs, so effortlessly, for long periods of time.

Louse Cage

This, of course, is one of the more flippant ways of referring to your hat, or perhaps, your friend's hat.

Lower than a Snake's Belly in a Wagon Rut

Are you feeling low? How low are you? You can't get much lower than a snake's belly in a wagon rut.

Lunch

Lunch, when that meal is not called dinner, is often the noon meal on the prairies. However, the term lunch is also used to mean food at a social event, no matter what time of day that event takes place. An invitation with the line "lunch will be served" indicates that you will be fed, be it afternoon, evening, or late night.

Many new arrivals to the West express surprise when, on certain social occasions, a meal is served at midnight. They express even greater surprise when the meal is called lunch. See also DINNER.

As in

Mirror, Alberta;
Mozart,
Saskatchewan;
Mallard, Manitoba

Mail-Order Cowboy

Mail-order cowboy is the real cowboy's contemptuous description of the evening and weekend cowboy—the fellow who has all the clothes, but who has never ridden a horse since his mother gave him a pony ride on his fifth birthday.

Makings

Your makings are your tobacco and cigarette papers for making roll-your-own cigarettes. In a day when smoking was the rule rather than the exception, store-bought cigarettes were for city slickers only. In the West you rolled your own, and if you were really good, you did it with one hand. See also BULL DURHAM.

Maria

Maria, along with linhead, or Red River pickerel, is a local term for that member of the cod family properly called burbot. This is a strange fish that looks like an eel and therefore is frequently rejected by fishermen despite all the assurance from others that it is delicious, especially smoked.

Mark Man

A person who cannot write and cannot sign his name, other than to make his mark with an X, is a mark man. When the term was in regular use, mark men were quite common and there was no great shame in admitting that you could not write or sign your name. At this time, there may be more individuals than most people realize who cannot write, but most of them can at least sign their names. However, if necessary, it is still legal to sign with an X if the making of the mark is properly witnessed.

Married in the Custom of the Country

See COUNTRY ALLIANCE.

Marsh Pump

Marsh pump is one of several names for the bittern. This one comes from the sound the bird makes as it stands among the reeds in the marsh. The sound it makes that led to this name is described in one bird book as "pomp-er-lunk." For another name and reported sound, see BUBBLY JUG. For yet another name see SHITEPOKE.

Matrimonial Cake

It is hard to believe anyone would call it anything else, but apparently elsewhere in the country the romantic-sounding matrimonial cake is reduced to the prosaic date squares.

McPhillips Street Station

McPhillips Street is in Winnipeg and there is not, and never was, a McPhillips Street Station—at least not a real one. McPhillips Street crosses the CPR main line, and during the Depression it was one of the locations in Winnipeg where men who were riding the rails hopped on and off trains. Two such locations picked up names.

When going to or arriving from the East on the CPR, you got on or off at the TRANSCONA DEPOT, which was, in fact, the eastern boundary of the Transcona rail yards. When going to, or arriving from, the West, you got on or off the train at the McPhillips Street Station—what was then a level crossing of McPhillips Street and the CPR line at the edge of the Weston rail yards. So, if you ever hear anyone speaking of boarding at the McPhillips Street Station you know that he was catching an unauthorized ride on a freight train.

Recently, the Manitoba Lotteries Commission built a casino close to what is now an underpass on McPhillips Street at the rail line and called it the McPhillips Station. It is interesting that a term for the spot were so many men got on, or off, a train in search of their fortune in terms of work and a little pay is now applied to a place where many more seek a much different fortune.

Meadow Muffins

Meadow muffins are what the cow leaves behind in the meadow. They can cause considerable mess when fresh. However, when thoroughly dried, they can be broken up into Cow Chips.

There is an old story of a Scottish farmer who lost his tam in the meadow when walking home in the dark. He tried on five before he found it.

Media Mafia

Westerners feel that the news and information media has been largely controlled by eastern Canada. While CanWest Global may be making some inroads, much of national television, news services, and, to a certain extent, radio, are centred in the East and tend to be controlled by Easterners. They seem to see and report things from only an Eastern perspective, and for this reason have been referred to as the media mafia by their Western counterparts.

Mess

A mess can mean a great many things on the prairies, including the condition of the kids' rooms. One very old, old country meaning of mess, which seems to be far more prevalent on the prairies than elsewhere, is a great amount. You can catch a mess of fish or get yourself into a mess of trouble.

Métis

The term Métis can be found in any dictionary, and while it is usually listed as a Canadian word, it is included here because the Métis are a people of the West. The term is French, meaning of mixed blood, and is used to identify those people of North American Indian and European (especially French) ancestry. Forming a culture distinct from either of their ancestral groups, at one time they laid claim to large areas of land in the Red, Assiniboine, and Saskatchewan River valleys.

Mitchif

Mitchif is a language that developed during the early days of the Métis in Rupert's Land. There are several dialects of Mitchif, the most common being a blend of French, English, and Cree. Other dialects resulted from the mixing of French and English with other First Nations languages, such as Salteaux. Mitchif is still alive and well, particularly in Saskatchewan, and is recognized as an important part of the Métis cultural heritage.

Moojuice

What else could moo juice be but milk?

Moosemilk

Originating in northern areas, moosemilk is used by many as a term for any potent liquor, mixed drink, or home brew. While the name moosemilk is applied to just about anything now, in the minds of many it is still a specific drink. It was, and still can be, a mixture of dark rum, water, and canned sweetened condensed milk, It tastes better than it sounds, but even if it didn't, water and canned milk were the only mixes available when, and where, this drink was first concocted.

That original recipe is now often modified to rum and milk, with the frequent addition of ice cream.

Mosey

This word is not just used in the movies—it has been, and still is, a part of the language of the West. Indicating a fairly leisurely movement, you can mosey off, mosey along, or simply mosey around.

Mossey Horn

A mossey hom is an old steer. When a steer reaches about five or six years of age, the base of its horns get corrugated and scabby in appearance and the animal becomes known as a mossey horn. The term may also be applied to people, so if you are called a mossey horn, either your old age, or aging attitude, is starting to show.

Mother Yeast

The mother yeast was another name for the sourdough kept to start each batch of bread. If the mother yeast was lost, the homesteader was unable to make bread and had to resort to bannock until more yeast, or another mixture of sourdough, was obtained. See also SOURDOUGH.

Mud

For most people, the first association with mud is simply the wet earth in which children love to play. However, throughout the oilpatch in Alberta and Saskatchewan, the first thing to come to mind would be the substance pumped as a packing material into wells as they are being drilled.

Mustang

A mustang is a horse descended from Spanish stock introduced into North America in the sixteenth century. For a time in the past, great numbers of wild mustangs roamed areas of the western United States, and to a lesser extent, western Canada. Being horses of renowned stamina and strength, mustangs were sought after for domestication, but were considered by many to be untameable. More commonly, a mustang is any wild horse, or even a horse that behaves in a wild and unruly manner.

As in

Nokomis, Saskatchewan; Narcisse, Manitoba; Nojack, Alberta

Nanny Whamming

Nanny whamming is the name for goat tying when performed as a rodeo event. As the term implies, it is not a serious competition event and is usually performed as entertainment by the young or by women. If done competitively, it will probably feature local youngsters vying for a small prize.

Women have been part of rodeos and Wild West shows since the days of Annie Oakley, but they have traditionally performed the entertainment events such as trick riding and shooting, leaving the main competition events to the men.

Nickel Large

A nickel large was the old five-cent package of five cigarettes, also known as fives. The price of cigarettes has changed rather dramatically from the days of five cents for five cigarettes.

Nicks and Kicks

Literally, your pants and shoes. But your nicks and kicks can refer to all your clothing. When, as a kid, you went skinny-dipping in the old swimming hole, you left your nicks and kicks in the bushes. See also KICKS.

Nip

Long before the advent of fast-food chains selling hamburgers by the millions, Winnipeg's twenty-four-hours-a-day, seven-days-a-week hamburger and general fast food outlets were the chain of Salisbury Houses. For whatever reason, Salisbury House has always called its hamburgers nips. Winnipeggers, especially the generation for whom Salisbury House was the only choice when looking for food in the wee small hours of the morning, still refer to nips when speaking of hamburgers. Ordering a nip and chips elsewhere can result in anything from a blank stare to a threat to call police.

Noble Blade

The Noble blade is actually a brand of plough, developed during the Dirty Thirties by C. S. Noble. He was originally from the United States, but spent most of his productive life on the Canadian prairies. The Noble blade slides under the surface of the soil without unduly disturbing the topsoil or trash cover, much like a large scuffler or Dutch hoe. The idea is to cut and kill the weeds in summerfallow without the need for traditional ploughing, thereby retaining moisture.

The idea of ploughing and cultivating is so ingrained that, to this day, unploughed fallow is often viewed with extreme skepticism.

North End Round

This is another Winnipeg expression, although other cities may well have similar sayings. Winnipeg's North End is known as the ethnic area of the city and, on the assumption that this area eats more bologna than steak, North End round is a name for bologna. Similar names for bologna exist that mention specific ethnic groups, such as Polish round or Ukrainian round.

At one time, a non-ethnic name for bologna was TUBE STEAK, but that term has now become associated with wieners.

Noseeums

Pronounced no see´ ums, these are virtually invisible biting insects. The bane of all who venture into the bush, these creatures are known across much of Canada, especially the northern treed areas, but they

were called noseeums in the Chinook jargon and they appear to be at their worst in the western bush.

With mosquitoes and black flies you can, at least, see the enemy. Not so when the noseeums attack. Inflicting pain far out of proportion to their size, they can drive an unprotected bush traveller to near frenzy.

Not so Big as a Bar of Soap After a Hard Day's Washing

Coined when washday involved tubs of water, a washboard, and a bar of soap, this is the time-honoured description of something very small.

Not Worth a Sack of Grain

Now here is an expression whose time, unfortunately, may have come again. During the Depression, things of little or no value were not worth a sack of grain. With the price of wheat what it is today, we may, sad to say, be hearing this expression again on the farms of western Canada.

For a while, in the 1950s especially, it was an expression that, while sometimes still used, had lost its original impact. Hopefully time will again render it inappropriate, but inappropriateness need not end its use. After all, many urban dwellers reflect on the expression dirt cheap despite the amount of the cheque they have to write for that little pile of topsoil they just had delivered to their front yard.

Nuggets

These nuggets are not made of gold; they are genuine frozen MEADOW MUFFINS. Nuggets are too large and too poor in quality to be used as hockey pucks. Horse manure makes far, far better hockey pucks! They can be used for Frisbees, but their aerodynamics is not the best. See also HOCKEY PUCKS.

Nuisance Ground/ Site

In one of the quainter euphemisms of the West, garbage dumps are called nuisance grounds. Well, they are a nuisance, aren't they?

As in

Otterburne, Manitoba; Onefour, Alberta; Oxbow, Saskatchewan

Oilpatch

The oilpatch refers to both a geographical area and an interest group. The oilpatch, therefore, is both the area where the oil industry is of major concern, and the industry itself. If something is beneficial or detrimental to the oilpatch, it will affect most of Alberta and parts of Saskatchewan, as well as all those associated with the oil industry within those areas.

On Boards

In many places, to go somewhere on skis has been traditionally referred to as going on the boards, or simply, on boards. That term goes back long before cross-country skiing was fashionable, to a time when your skis had probably been made in the shed from a couple of boards.

One Rooster Short of a Barnyard

To be one rooster short of a barnyard is much the same as being a FEW PICKLES SHORT OF A JAR.

One-way

Most people today would think only of street signs when they hear this term. To an older generation, a one-way was a disc harrow on which all the discs slanted in the same direction. A one-way could be handled by a team of horses as it pulled more easily than a harrow made up of opposing discs. The power of a tractor is required for the large, complex discs.

On the Range

This phrase, generally associated with Western songs and movies, actually has a definite meaning. Before the passage of HERD LAWS, cattle were allowed to roam on the open range. There was no requirement to fence in cattle in order to retain them on your own property. Cattle that were roaming freely were described as being on the range.

Open Heifer

An open heifer is one that is ready to breed, or simply a heifer in heat. The term open is used with other animals as well to indicate when they are in heat.

Opening a Field

Making the first round of a ripe field, whether it be with a combine or a swather, is the act of opening a field. Therefore, an opened field is one in which harvesting has begun, but has not yet been completed.

Out at the Seat

Out at the seat is the time-honoured way of referring to someone who is struggling financially.

Outfit

It has been suggested that the term outfit is the most useful word in a Western vocabulary—it can be used in so many ways that you need never fear running out of words to express yourself. Two of the most general uses are as follows.

1. In the days of the fur trade, the outfit was the supply of trading goods sent to an outpost for its trade. Once the traders received their outfit, they were outfitted for the year. From this, your outfit became the supplies required to undertake a journey or an endeavour. People still have to outfit themselves for a camping expedition.

2. Later, on the plains, an outfit was the ranch for which you worked. From this it became any company or business. You may say that someone finally got a job with a good outfit, or conversely, that someone is working for a Haywire outfit. It is one of those joyous terms that can cover just about any type of company imaginable from General Motors to the local candy store.

Outfitter

An outfitter was originally the one who provided the necessary equipment, or OUTFIT, either for an individual or an entire outfit. Now, outfitters not only provide the equipment and necessary goods for an expedition, but can organize and conduct an entire trail ride from a day to a couple of weeks. If you want to spend your holidays on horseback in the foothills or mountains, an outfitter will look after all your needs.

Out Gunning

If someone has gone hunting, the common expression in many parts of the West is simply to say that the person is out gunning, or even more commonly, out gunnin'. And why not? You can be out walking, out shopping, out riding, or out fishing, so why not out gunning?

Outhouse

Properly speaking, an outhouse is any building separated from the main building with which it has some functional connection. However, there will be few who do not make the immediate association with the BIFFY, at one time arguably the most important outhouse on the HOME QUARTER.

Outlaw

Apart from a criminal evading the law, an outlaw is a vicious horse that cannot be approached, let alone ridden. A cowboy could make a name for himself by breaking an outlaw, but frequently the bruises were not worth the effort. A broken outlaw could never be fully trusted as a working horse, so it was usually allowed to run wild. See also RANG-A-TANG.

Outriders

Originally, outriders rode separately, alongside the stage, wagon, or whatever it was they were accompanying. Frequently, they were armed outriders providing protection. Now, they are most commonly recognized as the four riders who load the stove into the chuckwagon and then must ride with the outfit to the finish line in a chuckwagon race at the rodeo.

Out the Side Door, Back Door, or Windshield

There are three directions in which you can get thrown off a bucking animal. You can go sideways or out the side door, you can go backwards or out the back door, or you can go over its head through the windshield. If you go out the side door from a bull, you do not want to fall into the WELL.

Overreach

See OVERSHOT.

Overseer

When reading the history of Saskatchewan towns and villages, you may come across the occasional reference to an individual called the town overseer. This might indicate that the community had suffered serious financial trouble, and a higher level of government had appointed an overseer to monitor current financial affairs. However, the overseer could either be an administrator appointed by a higher level of government when no mayor had been elected, or the name given to an individual chosen to act as a mayor in a community too small to warrant use of that term.

Overshot

An overshot horse is one that clicks its front hoof against its rear hoof when walking, a condition also known as OVERREACH.

Oversnow

Travel that would be considered overland in summer becomes oversnow in winter when undertaken by means designed to travel over the snow. This includes power toboggans or snowmobiles, skis, snowshoes, or dog sleds. See also SNOW PLANES and BOMBARDIER.

As in

Poe, Alberta; Pasqua, Saskatchewan; Pinawa, Manitoba

Padiddle

This, no doubt, is an expression of the past. Today's teenagers do not have to invent reasons to kiss someone. For their grandparents, however, things were different and little games were devised to create an acceptable situation for a kiss. This particular one involved the first person to see a car with only one working headlight. In a carload of teenagers, when the car with one light was sighted, you called out padiddle and touched the roof of the car. The first one to utter this magic word and remember to touch the roof got to kiss the person of his or her choice from among those in the car.

Heaven only knows why the word was padiddle. There may have been other terms used for the same game, but the one most frequently remembered is padiddle.

This game, utilizing padiddle or some other strange word, is reported elsewhere with varying rules. One variation turned the game into a form of strip poker played while driving. However, prairie residents reminiscing about padiddle considered it their game and will not admit to it ever going beyond kissing.

Pail Bunter

A pail bunter is the grain-fed calf of the barnyard cow. If you have ever seen a dog, or other family pet, start to knock its food dish around when the owner is deemed to be late with a meal, then you know the reason for expression. As the source of its food is the pail, these calves announce their hunger by giving it a few good bunts to catch someone's attention.

Pale Pink Red Cross

During World War II, the ladies of Teulon, Manitoba, wanted to form a helping organization along the lines of the Red Cross. For some reason, they did not want to form a chapter of the Red Cross, but still wished to contribute to the war effort. Therefore, they formed the Pale Pink Red Cross. Throughout the war, it contributed many of the services normally associated with the Red Cross.

Pancake Saddle

The Western rider who uses the heavy working saddle of the range views the light English saddle with absolute derision. One of the printable terms for the English saddle is pancake saddle.

Pan of Bread

A pan of bread consists of four loaves of bread baked together in the same pan. Bread baked this way must be pulled apart, like buns, resulting in loaves with soft sides. Perhaps somewhere, in some rural bakery, bread is still being baked four loaves to a pan and sold intact as a pan of bread, but it is most likely a thing of the past. It is quite possible that some homemade bread is still baked in four-loaf pans.

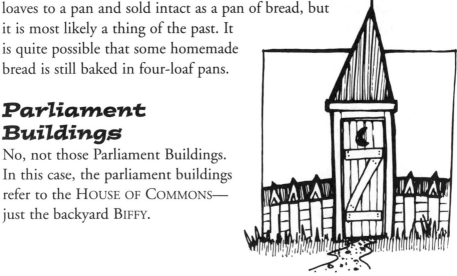

Parliament Buildings

No, not those Parliament Buildings. In this case, the parliament buildings refer to the HOUSE OF COMMONS— just the backyard BIFFY.

Patrol

The road grader that goes out and works the long, gravel prairie roads is known as a patrol. While the patrol could be referred to as being out on patrol, the term is more commonly used for the equipment itself. If you are looking for the operator of the equipment, you will be told that he is out on the patrol, not on patrol. The patrol could be out dragging the road for many days at a stretch. See also BLADE.

Pemmican

Pemmican is a mixture of dried ground meat and dried fruit and/or berries. It was the best nonperishable trail food available in the early West as it added the food value and taste of fruit and berries.

The Métis at Red River relied heavily on the pemmican trade, holding semi-annual buffalo hunts to get the meat and then selling the pemmican to the North West Company. See also JERKY.

Picking Rocks

This term means exactly what it says. It is the endless, thankless, back-breaking job of picking up the rocks that litter the farmland and which keep turning up out of the soil. While most farmers have some experience with picking rocks, others, such as those in the Manitoba Interlake, know it as a way of life. The term picking rocks, rather than picking up rocks, emphasizes the idea of the rocks being a crop growing in the prairie soil that has to be harvested. See also PRAIRIE APPLES and INTERLAKE POTATOES.

Picking Roots

Picking roots is another backbreaking job similar to picking rocks. It means to go across the farm picking up the chunks of root that have been turned up and cut off by the plough when virgin land has been brought into cultivation. While the roots were not as heavy as the rocks, they often had to be pulled out of the ground, making the work just as arduous.

Piece

It is reported from widely different areas of the prairies, especially where there was a strong Scottish influence, that the term piece was used to denote a small treat, goodie, or small snack. Children would pester grandma for a piece when they wanted one of the little treats that children often expect from grandmothers.

Piggin' String

A piggin' string is six-foot rope with a slip loop in one end that is used to tie the leg of a animal, usually a roped calf in the calf-roping contest at the rodeo. Therefore, it is the rope with which the cowboy ties a HOOEY.

Pinchers

Pinchers is the name given to the spruce beetle, an insect that can mistake people for trees. The spruce beetle bores into a spruce tree, so when it attacks a person it attempts to do exactly the same thing, causing excruciating pain. While spruce beetles are known across the continent, it is the northern prairies that call them pinchers.

Pit

Not just the gravel pit or any outside hole in the ground. The pit is also the hole in the ELEVATOR into which a farmer's grain is dumped so that it can be lifted up the LEG in order to be stored.

Pitch Bundles

To pitch bundles, or to be pitching bundles, is simply to be loading or unloading baled hay. Pitching hay would refer to the loads of loose hay that are not seen anymore. Pitching bundles is less common with the move to the newer large bales, which can only be moved with a forklift.

Pitch Woo

The expression to pitch woo has been widely used, but must surely have got its start in an area where pitching hay was a common occupation. If you could pitch hay you could pitch the words and actions of courtship as well. It is, therefore, to cuddle, smooch, or whatever you may call the actions of courtship that used to be called making love before that term assumed far greater meaning. The younger generation regards the term as far too quaint for its worldly sophistication.

Pit in

To pit in is to settle in for a long stay. The expression comes from settling into a goose pit or duck blind to begin the long wait. The prairie beer parlours used to close over the supper hour so that men could not pit in at the parlour after work and not get home for supper.

Pizen

Pronounced pie'zen, this is the rangeland pronunciation of poison. Like outfit and haywire, whether pronounced pizen or poison, its uses are far too numerous to list. It may be used to describe anything and everything you do not like, or anything that may be dangerous or harmful, even people, as in, "Steer clear of the likes of him; he's pizen."

Plough a Crooked Furrow

A farmer has always been judged by the straightness of the furrows he ploughs. If a man could not plough a straight furrow, you had reason to doubt his credibility. From this, to plough a crooked furrow has come to mean to lie, cheat, or be generally untrustworthy.

Plough Jockey

How can we heap abuse on a farmer? Let me count the ways! Plough jockey is another of those terms that began as a put-down or derogatory remark, but which has had much of the sting removed by many farmers taking the term and using it themselves, perhaps even with a sense of pride.

Plug-in

While, as elsewhere, electrical outlets on the prairies are generally called outlets, the outlet in the garage, beside the parking pad, in the parking lot, or wherever it exists for the primary purpose of plugging in your car in winter, is a plug-in, not an outlet. If, in winter, you run an extension to the outlet on the back wall of your house, that outlet suddenly becomes a plug-in. Come spring, when the extension is rolled up and put away, the plug-in magically reverts to an outlet.

Pocket

A pocket is grazing land that has only one entrance. It is of considerable value because stock grazing in a pocket cannot scatter from the area without passing through the easily monitored entrance.

Poor Man's Cadillac

Throughout western Canada, the common Chevrolet, or Chevy, has been known as the poor man's Cadillac. Do you remember the story of the Texan bragging to a Saskatchewan farmer about the size of his ranch? The Texan claimed that he could drive all day, from dawn to dusk, and still be on his own land. The Saskatchewan farmer replied simply, "Yep, had a truck like that once myself."

Porch Climber

Porch climber is another of the names by which the West has known its moonshine or home brew.

Porridge Drawer

Following a custom of their GO BACK LAND, many Scots, and others who learned the trick from them, would, from time to time, cook a huge pot of porridge. This was then poured into a container where it cooled and solidified. Chunks of this porridge could then be cut out and eaten, reheated or cold, over the following days as required. Chunks of cold porridge could even be carried out into the field to be eaten at noon. Frequently, the container used to store the porridge was one of the larger drawers under the kitchen counter, which then became known as the porridge drawer. One of the best porridge drawers, if you wanted a really big one, was the old tip-out flour bin that was once a part of most prairie kitchens.

Pothole

1. A pothole is a natural depression in the ground that collects runoff water, forming a natural water-storage area. Larger potholes provide a source of water for livestock and a home for migratory waterfowl. As there is no source of water other than runoff, smaller potholes can become stagnant or dry.

2. A pothole is also the hole left in a road by a FROST BOIL, a hole that can vary from small, insignificant things to car-destroying monsters. Like most prairie cities, Winnipeg fights a losing battle with frost boils, and their offspring, the pothole, every spring. Some give the city the dubious claim of being called Pothole Capital of the World. In an effort to deal with this very real problem that can do serious damage to paved roads and the cars that use them, Winnipeg established a pothole hotline so that citizens can keep the public works crews informed as to where the latest problem exists.

   The only people who like potholes are the auto mechanics that earn a living doing front-end alignments.

Poverty Box

The poverty box was a box attached to a mower to catch the heads of grain that got cut off too short to be retained when the cut crop was swathed. It is impossible not to have some loss when harvesting, but anything that adds to the retained crop assists in the prevention of poverty.

Prairie Apples

Prairie apples are the smaller stones that keep turning up, year after year, as the land is worked. In fact, the land does not have to be worked to produce them, as they tend to appear every spring without assistance. They are also known as potatoes, especially in Manitoba's Interlake area. Both terms, apples and potatoes, come from the size of the rocks and the feeling that they must be growing in the ground. See also INTERLAKE POTATOES and PICKING ROCKS.

Do not, of course, confuse prairie apples with ROAD APPLES, which are something very different.

Prairie Chicken

Properly called the greater prairie chicken (*Tympanucbus cupido*) this bird has graced many prairie supper tables (along with those impostors, the sharp-tailed grouse and ruffed grouse), both as a matter of necessity and as a matter of choice.

Not known as being among the world's smartest birds, they are not only good eating, they are also relatively easy to shoot. This no doubt contributed to the greater prairie chicken becoming an endangered species. Indeed, for a while they were feared to be extinct, but recently their numbers seem to have made a modest recovery.

The male greater prairie chicken can put on a magnificent dancing display, not to be confused with the drumming of the ruffed grouse, sometimes called a prairie chicken. The ruffed grouse's drumming sound is made by beating the air with his wings and is best described as the sound of a distant motor starting and gaining speed. These drumming and dancing displays attract females while warning off other males.

Prairie Dog

Best known in southern Saskatchewan, these burrowing rodents live communally, sometimes by the hundreds, in what are properly called towns. While cute as can be when seen in the zoo, prairie dogs are not so cute when they are tearing up the landscape to create a new town on your farm. See also TOWNS.

Prairie Fires

See BURN.

Prairie Giant

Prairie giant is a common reference to the country elevator that stands, or at least used to stand, so tall above its surroundings, in thousands of communities across the West. See also ELEVATOR.

Prairie Oyster

1. A prairie oyster may be a glass of beer into which a raw egg has been broken. This meaning is known across a larger area than the Canadian prairies, but the next two are unique to the West.

2. In Saskatchewan, a prairie oyster may be a cracker with a ring of butter around the outside. Inside this ring of butter is a large dollop of ketchup with, perhaps, a dab of Worcestershire sauce in the middle of that. This little snack also goes under the name of SASKATCHEWAN COCKTAIL.

3. The real prairie oysters are the testicles of farm animals, preferably bull calves, which have been prepared for eating. These culinary delights are also known as BULL FRIES.

Prairie Sailors

During World War II, an extremely high proportion of the men joining the Royal Canadian Navy came from the prairies. Ever since then, there has been a disproportionate number of men and women, prairie born and bred, serving in Canada's navy. No one really knows why this is. It has been suggested that the farm boy has walked enough in his life and views the sea as a new experience, therefore joining the navy instead of the army. It has also been suggested that there was not a great deal of difference between sitting on a tractor looking at wheat fields stretching to the horizon and sitting on a ship looking at water stretching to the horizon. (Whoever came up with that one should get seasick on a

tractor!) Whatever the reason, these men and women formed a very proud group of prairie sailors. In 1985, when the Canadian navy celebrated its seventy-fifth anniversary, one of the largest reunions was held in Winnipeg, about as far from either coast as you can get.

Prairie Schooner

This term was used far more commonly in the United States, but it was not unknown on the Canadian plains. A prairie schooner was the great covered wagon that sailed the prairie seas bringing out the early settlers. In western Canada, the RED RIVER CART was seen, and heard, more frequently than the prairie schooner.

Prairie Sentinel

Prairie sentinel is another apt term by which we know that symbol of the prairies, the country elevator. See also ELEVATOR and PRAIRIE GIANT.

Prairie Sunset

While this is a natural phenomenon rather than a term or expression, nowhere will you witness sunsets to match those seen on the Canadian prairies. Filling the sky with glorious colour, these sunsets have awed all who have seen them. The magnificence of a prairie sunset may be partly due to meteorological conditions, but it also owes much to the incredible sweep of prairie horizon over which the display is spread. To blush like a prairie sunset is to blush the most brilliant shades of red humanly possible.

Prairie Wildflowers

What more nauseatingly cute term could you think of for pretty, young prairie girls than prairie wildflowers? Oh well, you can be sure they would choose prairie wildflower over good-looking heifer, but would, no doubt, prefer that neither be used.

Prairie Wool

Prairie wool is a type of short prairie grass that once covered much of the Western plains. This short, curly grass, when mowed, clung together like sheared lamb's wool, thereby gaining the name prairie wool. It had a number of uses and was very nutritious as a feed.

Principal Meridian

The Principal Meridian, or WINNIPEG MERIDIAN, is the first north–south meridian from which the great survey of the West began. The Principal Meridian is located at 97°27′28″.41 West longitude and crosses the trans-Canada highway just west of Winnipeg, near Headingly.

If, when headed west on the trans-Canada highway, you look to your right just after passing the Headingly weigh station, you will see a cairn which sits on the Principal Meridian and commemorates the start of the great DOMINION LANDS SURVEY.

Prove up

To prove up was to meet the requirements necessary to gain title to the land granted as a homestead under the terms of the Homestead Act. The term is a corruption of the original requirement that the homesteader improve the homestead. These requirements were to clear a minimum of ten acres a year for three years and to build a residence on the land. If you met these two requirements, you had proved up and were thus entitled to receive full title to the land.

To this day, the expression can be used to express the idea of meeting the requirements laid down to achieve a certain goal.

Pull Leather

To pull leather is to grab hold of some part of the saddle while riding a bucking horse. When done during a saddle-bronc riding competition at a rodeo, it results in disqualification. As with so many terms, it tends to come into wider use, in this case meaning to grab onto something, literally or figuratively, to gain support. See also GRABBING THE APPLE.

Pull the Pin

This is really a railroading term, as it comes from dropping off a boxcar by pulling the pin that locks the connecting knuckle. To pull the pin, however, appears to be used frequently in the West as an expression meaning to leave, quit, take off, or in some way disassociate yourself from someone or something.

Push Binder

Just as it suggests, a push binder was a binder that, instead of being pulled, was pushed from behind by a team. While it sounds awkward, it served a useful purpose. Equipment that is pulled must be offset to one side to keep the horses out of the uncut grain. This results in a certain loss of effective pulling power. By putting the team behind the binder, they could be centered on the equipment and yet not be trampling uncut crop.

As in

Quantock,
Saskatchewan;
Quadra, Manitoba;
Queenstone, Alberta

Quarter

Quarter is simply short for quarter section. A quarter section is half-a-mile by half-a-mile square, or 160 acres. Small to mid-size farms may be described by the number of quarter sections they contain. Large farms would be described in terms of sections. See also DOMINION LANDS SURVEY.

Quarter Horse

The quarter horse was originally bred for thoroughbred racing on a quarter-mile track. Because of its speed and agility, it has become renowned as the finest working horse, or COW HORSE, on the range.

Quarter Lines

Quarter lines are the lines that mark the division of a SECTION into quarter sections. Commonly referred to as the half-mile line, a quarter line is of no great consequence on most farms and, as it is not marked by any boundary such as a road allowance, it is only noticeable if it happens to form the dividing line between two crops, or perhaps the division between two properties.

Queen's Mutton

The Queen's mutton is illegal venison or other major game, especially that which was shot on Crown land—which explains the reference to the

Queen. Why it is mutton is anybody's guess. The term probably is a variation on the English expression Queen's, or King's, venison, which is poached game.

Queen's mutton is not to be confused, however, with GOVERNMENT BEEF/MEAT—either deer or rabbit—usually obtained legally, unlike Queen's mutton.

As in

Reykjavik, Manitoba; Rosebud, Alberta; Reward, Saskatchewan

Rabbit Berries

These are a very small counterpart to buffalo chips—rabbit berries are rabbit droppings. Their size and shape justify the name.

Rabbit Drive

Everyone has heard of cattle drives, but not everyone is aware that there were also rabbit drives on the prairies. During the late 1800s and early 1900s, rabbits could be a very real problem. It was not just a problem of excessive numbers and damaged crops. The big prairie fires of the 1800s meant that most tree growth was very young and easily damaged by rabbits looking for food in winter. Communities, therefore, organized rabbit drives in which beaters with sticks swept an area, driving the rabbits into a fenced enclosure where they were clubbed or shot to death. In this way, the rabbit population was brought under control.

While some of the rabbits may have been used for meat, the main idea of the rabbit drive was to control numbers, not to obtain food. Today's animal rights groups would not be pleased with the thought of these rabbit drives, but the early farmers saw it very much as a matter of survival.

Radiator Hooch

During the Depression and World War II, and for many people even after that, antifreeze was either unavailable or too expensive. The only

alternative to antifreeze during a
prairie winter was to drain the
radiator every night. To avoid
this nuisance, cheap moonshine
was purchased and used in place
of antifreeze. Particularly harsh
moonshine, which was really
only good for use as antifreeze,
was called radiator hooch.

Rake
To rake a horse is to use your spurs aggressively. See also SCRATCHING.

Rail Jack
A rail jack is a mechanical device that allows one person to move a
loaded grain car. Use of a rail jack allowed for SPOTTING of grain cars at
the ELEVATOR between visits by the TRAMP.

Ranch
While the term ranch is not unique to western Canada by any stretch of
the imagination, it definitely has a Western connotation. Coming from
the Spanish word *rancho*, which means a group of people eating together,
a ranch is an animal breeding and raising enterprise most commonly
associated with cattle. While the term is commonly used in reference to
the land, the fact that it is really the enterprise explains all the other
breeding and raising enterprises that use the term as well, such as a
mink ranch.

Rancher
A rancher was not only the owner of a ranch, but also a small stove with
a little oven in the base of the stovepipe.

Rang-a-tang
Also heard in some areas as rangy-tang, rang-a-tang means wild,
untamed, or even crazy. Used originally to describe wild horses, the term
has come to be applied to people as well. See also OUTLAW.

Range

1.   For ranchers, the range is the land on which the cattle are kept. While the term is applied to the land area, it actually derives from the roaming, or ranging, of the cattle. Your range is the land on which your cattle can range. See also HERD LAWS.

2.   For farmers, the first association with range might well be of a range of townships. A range is a north-south row of townships. A TOWNSHIP is identified by the number of townships that it is north of the border in a given range. That range is identified by the number of ranges that it is east or west of the PRINCIPAL MERIDIAN, or west of the second through sixth meridians. As these are survey terms, for further information see DOMINION LANDS SURVEY.

Rebchuckism

A tortured or totally butchered expression, properly called a malapropism, is a Rebchuckism to many Winnipeg residents. The name comes from Slaw Rebchuck, a former Winnipeg city councillor who was forever using such expressions. He claimed that having discovered the attention attracted by these twisted sayings, he deliberately created more of them. It always appeared, however, as if they were just Slaw Rebchuck's way of speaking, and it made him famous. Following are a few contributions to the English language attributed to him.

"We're in total darkness but I can see the light."

"Let's get it in black and writing."

"This agenda shouldn't take long; there's nothing contagious on it."

Redeye

Redeye is a glass of beer with tomato juice in it. As it is properly called CALGARY REDEYE, see further comments under that name and TWO AND A JUICE.

Red River Cart

The Red River cart was the moving van of the prairies during the early days. It was a fairly small, strong cart with two large wheels and was pulled by oxen or horses. The wooden wheels fitted directly onto wooden axles that were not greased, as grease would just collect dust and dirt and wear out the axle. The rubbing of wood on wood meant that these carts could be heard coming miles away. The vast number of these carts that crossed the West carved deep ruts into the prairie soil.

The next time you drive the trans-Canada highway through Saskatchewan, stop at the picnic grounds on the north side of the highway at the junction with Highway 201, just east of Broadview. A cairn marks a spot where you can see the ruts carved by the wagons and Red River carts of the early pioneers on one of the main routes west. Unfortunately, while the site is marked, it is unprotected, so what were once highly visible ruts are being quickly worn away.

Remittance Men

At one time when the son of a well-to-do English family needed to be banished from home for some reason (usually involving a real or perceived blot on the family name), western Canada was one of the places he might be sent. These men were supported by a regular allowance, or remittance, from home that for many of them was sufficient enough that they did not need to seek work. These individuals became known as remittance men.

Riding the Fence

Quite apart from Zane Grey novels, a very real job was, and still is, to ride along the fence to find and repair places where the cattle can get through. While it is derived from this literal riding along the line of a fence, the expression can also be used for any job that involves figurative fence mending, or checking for problems. A salesperson, therefore, out solving problems and generally keeping customers happy, is riding the fence.

Riding the Varnish

In the days when riding the rails was common, riding the varnish was to hitch a ride on a passenger train. This was difficult and dirty as the only place on a passenger train was behind the engine in, or around, the coal car. There you could be easily seen and removed, even after you were as black as the coal. The only advantage to riding the varnish, when it was achieved, was that it was a much faster trip than a ride on a freight train.

The term riding the rails was coined in the United States during the Depression and initially involved putting boards across the rails under a boxcar and riding on them. In Canada it was most likely that the ride was in an empty boxcar. But the expression became known right across the continent no matter how the ride was accomplished, with the rails coming to mean the track rails rather than the boxcar rails. See also Side-door Pullman.

Rigging

A rodeo cowboy's gear and working equipment required for the various rodeo events is his rigging, or, more likely, his riggin'.

Rigging Bag

If rigging is the cowboy's gear, then the bag he keeps it in is his rigging, or riggin', bag.

Road Allowance

Perhaps the Western pronunciation of this word is more unique than the meaning. The road allowance is the strip of public land between townships and sections that is reserved for the construction of roads. At the beginning of the Dominion Lands Survey, the road allowance was one-and-a-half chains, or ninety-nine feet. (That is 30.1752 metres, if you really must know.) Later it was reduced to one chain, or sixty-six feet (20.1168 metres).

Throughout the West you will seldom hear the term road allowance used. What you will hear, time and time again, is reference to the Roadlounce, which happens to be the same thing.

Road Apples

One does not encounter road apples as much as one used to as these are the droppings left by horses. For many of the younger generation, the only association with road apples will be the clowns with shovels and bags who work the parades that feature horses. Frozen road apples are Hockey Pucks or Horse Puckies, so see also those terms.

In the days when delivery vans were pulled by horses, even city streets had their share of road apples. When trucks replaced horse-drawn delivery wagons, many people complained about the loss of free fertilizer that they had previously gathered off the street.

Very little, if any, of that free fertilizer came from the horses pulling delivery vans for the T. Eaton Co. The horses used by Eaton's were kept on a feeding cycle that ensured that they did not defecate on the city streets, only in their own barns.

Roadeo

No, it is not misspelled. A roadeo is a competition between truckers, rather than cowboys. Just as the rodeo tests the skills of the cowboy, so the roadeo tests the driving skills of truckers. With points awarded in each of the individual skill tests involving maneuvering and backing up, the operator with the highest point total is the roadeo champion.

Roadlounce

Roadlounce is the correct, proper, and normal way for western Canadians to pronounce ROAD ALLOWANCE.

Road Pizza

Definitely a more modern term than road apples, road pizzas are all those squashed animals, commonly called roadkill, that you see along the highway.

Rocks

BUTTES tend to be called rocks by Westerners—even those composed of earth and clay, as they usually are.

Rodeo

A rodeo is a competition among cowboys in events growing out of the traditional skills of their work. Actually, in many events it is the cowboy and his horse that participate in the competition, just as the two of them work together as a team on the range.

Rodeo comes from the Spanish word *rodear*, that means to surround. In a rodeo, the cowboy works within a surrounded or fenced area, rather

than out on the open plain. Somewhere along the line, the rodeo
has also picked up the name stampede, as in the Calgary Stampede.
See also STAMPEDE.

Root Rake

A root rake, as one might surmise, is a large-toothed rake dragged
through the soil to remove tree roots from virgin land after the stumps
have been pulled and the sod busted.

Rubbing Stone

Many animals that shed in the spring rub up against objects to assist in
the shedding process. Most use trees to rub against as, no doubt, did the
buffalo, when and if they could find a tree big enough. On the BALD
PRAIRIE, however, there were occasional large stones that provided the
surface against which these massive beasts could scrape off their heavy
winter hair. These are the rubbing stones of the West. The ground
around the stones was pounded down into a deep track by the passage
of thousands of buffalo. At one time, if you wanted buffalo hair for any
purpose, you could get all you wanted at a rubbing stone.

These rubbing stones can still be viewed, but they are often on
private property, which makes access to them difficult. However, a few
are accessible. One is displayed at the Fort Whyte Centre in Winnipeg,
but it was moved from its original location so it does not have the
packed path of the buffalo around it.

Russian Peanuts

See UKRAINIAN PEANUTS and SPITS.

Rustle

Not the stealing of cattle, but rather the action of getting grass from
beneath the snow. Cattle must rustle grass in the winter, if not being
fed, as must all wild foraging animals. From this, it has come to mean
to provide food and, from there, to prepare food for eating. Therefore,
rustling up the grub can either refer to bringing home the bacon or
cooking the meal.

As in
Stand Off, Alberta; Saltcoats, Saskatchewan; Sundance, Manitoba

Saddle Tramp

The term saddle tramp is the original Western description of a person of no fixed address, whose home was literally the saddle. The expression is still heard today, as it may be applied to wandering, itinerant workers in range country. See also TUMBLEWEED.

Sangwiches

The extent of this pronunciation is unclear, but there are prairie people to this day (and there used to be a lot more of them), who take a couple of sangwiches to work in their lunch pail.

Saskatchewan Cocktail

Saskatchewan cocktail is another name for a cracker with butter, ketchup, and Worcestershire sauce. This is also one of the definitions of a PRAIRIE OYSTER.

Saskatchewan Grunt

Somewhere along the way, apparently out in Nova Scotia, a fruit dish with a covering of dough, properly called a cobbler, picked up the name grunt. However, when made on the prairies with Saskatoon berries, the name of the dish becomes Saskatchewan grunt.

Saskatoons

Actually a member of the rose family, the Saskatoon (*Amelanchier alnifolia*) can be found across western Canada. The purple berries are delicious, as any Westerner can tell you, and are used extensively for pies and preserves, as well as for eating just as they come off the bush.

Saskatoons can be purchased from any of the numerous vendors along major highways but many Westerners still prefer to pick their own, if at all possible. Many families have their favourite berry-picking spot to which they return year after year. But, be careful. Saskatoons are favoured by many species and the funny grunting noise behind you may not be a companion eating while picking, but a bear who is just as intent on berry picking as you are.

School Section

As detailed under DOMINION LANDS SURVEY, every township in the original survey had two sections set aside as the school sections. These were normally sections 11 and 29, unless either or both of these sections were totally unsuitable. The idea was to sell all or most of this land to raise money for the construction and maintenance of a schoolhouse. A small portion of land might be retained for the actual site of the school, if that was convenient.

As the school sections could vary greatly in value from township to township, it resulted in wide differences in the amount of money available for schools.

Scotch Rope

Do the Scots really deserve their reputation for thrift? This is a term that is based on the assumption that they do, as Scotch rope is the familiar closure of a box by weaving the four flaps together so that it stays closed without real rope. Really, of course, the term should be Scot's rope as any Scotsman will tell you that Scotch is a drink, not a person from Scotland. However, as expressions do not always follow correct English usage, Scotch rope it is.

Scratching

Scratching is another term that refers to applying spurs to the horse. Scratching is generally considered to be a more gentle use of the spurs than RAKING.

Screening

Screening is simply the method of cleaning grain by passing it over a vibrating screen that carries off the larger kernels of wild oats and other impurities, while allowing the grain to fall through. See also CARTER DISK.

Screenings

Screenings are the weed seeds and other bits and pieces that are separated from the grain when it is cleaned by screening. When a farmer has grain cleaned for use as seed, the screenings may be received back, as they are mainly wild oats that can be used for cattle feed.

From this, screenings may be anything left over after a cleaning or sorting out process. When you are carefully picking over fruit for preserving, that which is good enough to eat but not to go into the jar, gets put aside for immediate consumption. These are a form of screenings and are sometimes referred to as such.

Scrub

A scrub, sometimes called a float, was a heavy platform dragged over newly broken land to break up the large clumps of turned sod and level the land.

Scrubbing

Scrubbing is another name for BRUSHING, the act of cutting bush when clearing land. This work would tend to be called scrubbing where the term scrub brush was in common usage; otherwise it was simply brushing.

"That which we call a rose by any other name would smell as sweet" and clearing land, no matter what the term used to describe it, was back-breaking work when done without modern equipment.

Scrub Brush

This is not only what is used to clean the kitchen floor. A dictionary will define scrub as low, stunted trees and shrubs. In western Canada, the term scrub brush refers to areas of small trees with a lower tangle of bushes and shrubs.

Scrub Game

A scrub game may appear as unorganized as the confusion of growth in scrub brush, but it often has dozens of rules, many made up on the spot that day, but all known and obeyed by all players. It is a game played without formal sides or teams, where players can come and go as they must, but the game carries on. Scrub hockey accommodates all who want to play. In scrub baseball, the number of players present at any given time play through a succession of positions, without being divided into teams. A set number of players, normally no less than four, are at bat and remain so until they are out. When they have been put out, they go to the outfield to work their way back in again through all the positions. The number of positions can be far more numerous than in a real game as all players, once regular positions have been filled, are accommodated in the field.

Scrub games are seldom seen in this day and age of formal leagues, with rule books, umpires, coaches, governing bodies, and adults in control of everything.

Scuffle/Scuffler

To scuffle is to cultivate land by cutting the weeds off just below the surface of the ground, without digging or turning the surface soil. In the vegetable garden, this form of cultivation is different from hoeing. It is often associated with the potato patch, with many adults remembering being sent out as children to scuffle the potatoes, usually with a small scuffler that was often called a Dutch hoe.

When done on a large scale on the farm land, it was accomplished with an implement called a scuffler, the best known of which was the NOBLE BLADE.

Scunnered

To be scunnered is to be cheated, beaten, or bested in some way. To take a scunner is to leave without paying the bill or meeting a financial obligation. Therefore, if you took a scunner and left the restaurant without paying your bill, the restaurant and waiter were scunnered. It is the equivalent of the current, more widely used expressions see off, seen off, and been seen off. It is an adaptation of the Scottish word *scunner* that is used in reference to someone who has got the better of you in some way and who is, therefore, disliked.

Section

One of the basic terms used in the survey of the West, a section is one thirty-sixth of a township, or one square mile of land. It equals 640 acres, or 258.99 hectares (commonly accepted as 259 hectares).

Each township is a square, six sections by six sections and the thirty-six sections are numbered beginning at the southeast corner and progressing west across the southern row, then east across the next row to the north and then back and forth until you reach section thirty-six in the northeast corner. See also DOMINION LANDS SURVEY.

Section 37

As there are thirty-six sections in a township, section 37 does not exist. You may, however, hear an occasional reference to this non-existent land. If, for instance, you see your friend with a nice load of wood, gravel, sand, or some such commodity, you may well ask where he got it. If he answers that he got it from section 37, ask no more questions. Wherever it was that he found it, he should not have been there.

The fictional section 37 can also be used to send the greenhorn off on a wild goose chase. Just as the sailor sends the naive newcomer off to get a sky hook, so the rural dweller, having grown tired of silly questions from the city slicker or Easterner, may well send him off in search of section 37.

See a Man About a Horse/Dog

Originating in a far more inhibited time, to see a man about a horse, or about a dog, was one of the polite ways to refer to going to the BIFFY, and later, the bathroom. After all, when asked where she was going, your grandmother would not have said that she was going to the bathroom.

This very quickly became an expression meaning simply that, wherever you were going, or whatever you were doing, it was no one else's business. Today, therefore, it is simply a means to avoid answering a question without saying, "It's none of your business." See also GOING TO SEE THE PRAIRIE BEARS.

Seeing Daylight

Seeing daylight, or to see daylight, is when the rider in a bucking competition leaves the saddle so that daylight can be seen between the rider and the saddle. It does not necessarily mean that the rider is being thrown and it does not cause disqualification, as with GRABBING THE APPLE, but it does add some excitement to the ride.

Semack

Semack is an expression heard in various parts of the prairies to mean soon, especially where it is a single-word answer: "When will you get back?" "Semack!" The expression likely comes from the Bungay word *chimmuck*, meaning soon or sudden.

Sentinel

See PRAIRIE SENTINEL.

Separator

1. The first association with separator, for most Westerners, will be the cream separator. They are not seen often now, as fewer grain farmers keep cows, but they were a standard part of farms not so long ago. After keeping cream wanted by the family, the remainder was sold to the local dairy. See CREAM CHEQUE.
2. Before the jobs of cutting and threshing were performed by one machine—the combine—the threshing machine was also called a separator.

Shagannappi

Shagannappi was the name given to raw buffalo hide and, occasionally, to articles made with that hide. In the days when buffalo hunts still took place, shagannappi was used for harness and all leather accoutrements.

Shagannappi was also used to provide a type of tire on the wooden wheels of the Red River ox cart. A strip of raw buffalo hide wrapped around the wooden rim of the wheel shrunk as it dried, forming a tight, durable covering. The shagannappi did not improve the ride of the cart, but it was easily replaced when necessary and preserved the wooden wheel indefinitely.

Shaking Like a Wet Weed

This expression is also heard as shivering like a wet weed. Do wet weeds shake or shiver? They certainly do during a rain and can continue to do so afterwards as the drops of rain run off. Perhaps it is, however, only a variation on the more popular saying, shaking like a leaf.

Sheaf

A sheaf is a bunch of wheat tied together for handling. A group of standing sheaves becomes a STOOK. For many people today, the only time they will see a sheaf of wheat is in a picture or at church at Harvest Thanksgiving where the tied sheaf is the neatest way to represent that aspect of the harvest.

She Didn't Pretty Much

Apparently originating in Alberta, she didn't pretty much means that a woman is rather plain. It does not suggest ugliness, just an absence of notable beauty. This is an intriguing expression as it treats beauty in an unusual way, as if it is something that happens to people over time and in this case didn't.

Apparently, he didn't handsome much was not a term applied to all the men who deserved it.

Shelterbelt

The shelterbelt is the ring of trees around a farmyard, or the row of trees beside a field, designed to provide protection from the wind and snow. When we drive across the prairies today, it may appear to us that every farmer was lucky enough to find a beautifully treed area in which to build the house and barn. In truth, of course, these treed areas have been carefully grown over several generations. Before that, the area was as bald as the rest of the prairie. Before shelterbelts grew big enough to break the wind, the farm buildings themselves caught the full effect of the wind and weather. There are accounts of drifts up to the roof of the barn after blizzards, requiring the farmer to chop a hole in the roof of the barn to get to the animals.

Shitepoke

Shitepoke, or shikepoke, is another name for the bittern, along with MARSH PUMP and BUBBLE JUG. While the latter two names are based on the noise these birds make, it is unclear where the term shitepoke originated. It may have something to do with its appearance as it stands in the ditch trying, very successfully, to look like a reed or stick.

Shoat

Shoat is the term for a pig that is a little older than a sucker but not old enough to be a sow or boar. It is, therefore, a young pig that is old enough to feed itself.

Shoot the Luck

How many ways did our ancestors have for avoiding language that would have been considered crude? When the word darn was risky and damn unthinkable, shoot the luck was a polite way to register the same feeling. While it is seldom heard anymore in its entirety, it is still heard as simply, shoot! The present younger generation probably believes that shoot is a polite replacement for a frequently uttered expletive used by them, and so it is, but not as directly as they may think.

Shovel Leaners

Among those who believe, rightly or wrongly, that they work twice as hard as public employees, all railway work crews, road crews, or any other workers frequently seen resting on their shovels in the public view, are known as shovel leaners. Within those groups themselves, the term may be used to describe one of their number who manages to do the least amount of labour possible.

All those who work in public view are subject to criticism regarding the intensity of their work and the length of their coffee breaks. There are many jokes based on the belief that they do not really work up a sweat. There is an old familiar complaint that, "They should put rope handles on those tools!" And an old riddle: "What is yellow and sleeps three?" Answer: "A public works three-quarter ton."

Show a Flag

The flag is the white rear underside of a white-tailed deer. This is clearly seen when the deer runs away, or shows its flag. The flashing of the white flag is believed to be a warning sign to other deer. Therefore, to show your flag, or a flag, is to run away.

Shribles

Shribles is a mixture of cooked macaroni and stewed tomatoes. It is one of those easily made meals, the kind that those who are strangers to the kitchen can make all by themselves. It is a variation on bacon and beans, or simply beans, the other simple, cook-for-yourself dinners.

In the memoirs of bachelor homesteaders there are frequent references to Sunday being the day for sharpening the plough and making a big pot of beans and bacon that would provide dinners for the next week. If macaroni and canned tomatoes had been available, they might have cooked shribles once in a while for a change.

Side-door Pullman

When hitching a ride on a freight train, to ride in an empty boxcar is to travel in a side-door Pullman. Of course, this expression requires knowledge of what a Pullman is before it can be appreciated. Unfortunately, many of the younger generation have had no experience with a Pullman, or railway sleeping car.

Side-hill Gougers

These are mythical creatures with short legs on one side and long legs on the other that once lived in the Qu'Appelle Valley. They are responsible for the odd gouges or furrows that mark the steep slopes of the valley; marks they made as they foraged their way down the Qu'Appelle, moving along the valley with ease, their short legs on the upper part of the slope and their long legs on the lower.

Sad to say, they all perished. When they got to the end of the valley and turned around to go back, their short legs were on the low side of the hill and their long legs on the high side, and they rolled down the hill and died.

Side of the House

Side of the house is an expression heard in many parts of the West that simply means side of the family, as in, "He gets his big ears from your side of the house."

Sin and Misery

1. During the Depression, when there was no money for real coffee, a coffee of sorts was made from whatever was handy. Usually it was ground wheat, with the possibility of other added ingredients. Known by many names, mostly unprintable, it was widely recognized as sin and misery—it being a sin to waste the wheat and misery to drink the coffee.

2. Despite hard times, sin and misery is not being perked in farmhouse kitchens any more. But it remains in another form. Some prairie women report that old sin and misery is still there, but in the shape of a husband—it being a sin to leave the old codger and misery to live with him.

Sinkhole

Sinkholes are small depressions in the prairies, often with an alkaline well below. Conditions at the sinkhole vary with the water level and one day they can be bone dry and hard, while on another they are wet and cattle may sink in and become mired down. However, it is not the sinking of cattle that gives it the name; it is the deepening of the holes as the alkaline well washes away earth.

Siwash

A Siwash is the familiar heavy wool sweater, usually homemade. On the West Coast it would be called a Cowichan, while in the East it would apparently be known as a Mary Maxim.

Siwash is actually a Chinook word for Indian.

Skid Boots

Skid boots are protective leather boots put on a horse's fetlocks to prevent it skinning or burning itself when skidding to a fast stop. They are most commonly seen on horses ridden in rodeo events where such fast skidding stops are required, but they are also worn by cutting horses working cattle on the range.

Skiff

While our friends on either coast might think first of a small boat, the real skiff is a light dusting of something, most commonly snow. That light layer of dry snow blowing across the surface of the landscape is a skiff of snow. The term may also be heard in other similar situations, such as placing a skiff of flour in a pan.

Skinny Ass

Skinny ass is a way of riding a horse. To be riding skinny ass is to be riding bareback. That means, of course, that the horse's back is bare, not the rider's. In this day and age, one can make no assumptions in such matters.

Sleepers

A sleeper may be a railroad tie or even a railroad sleeping car for some, but it is also a stone that is just below the surface of the land and therefore out of sight until struck and turned up by the plough. This word goes along with GRINNERS and STROLLERS, the rocks just showing through the ground and those on top. Sleepers are the worst of the three as they cannot be seen when ploughing. Striking a sleeper can blunt or damage the plough, and when the farmer was walking behind the FOOT BURNER it could throw the plough out of the ground.

See also PRAIRIE APPLES and INTERLAKE POTATOES.

Sleepy-R

Reference to the Sleepy-R is a reference to the CPR (Canadian Pacific Railway) in less than complimentary terms. It has the multiple impact of being a takeoff on the sound of the letters CPR, an assessment of the energy of CPR workers (an assessment they would claim rightfully belonged only to the CNR), while also sounding like a Western cattle brand. See also SHOVEL LEANERS.

Slewing

The word slew can be defined as turning or swinging around on an axis. You can slew around in your chair to see who has come up behind you.

When applied to the motion of the car, it is generally used to mean a spinning turn, such as is made when you brake sharply while turning the wheel, so as to end up facing the opposite direction. In the West, slewing is the fishtailing motion of a car on a muddy or icy road, or a road covered in loose gravel.

Slick

A slick is an animal that is old enough to have been branded, but which has no brand. In the days of the open range a slick, too old to be following an identifiable mother, belonged to whoever caught it and branded it.

Slip

In the days of horse-drawn earth-moving and road-building equipment, a slip was an earthmover pulled by two horses.

Slough

Here is a word, the pronunciation of which, if not the use, will brand you a western Canadian without any doubt. Pronounced to rhyme with shoe, not plough, this is the term for a generally wet, low-lying area that floods during heavy rain or spring runoff. At other times, it may be marshy, muddy, or perhaps even dry, depending on weather conditions. However, sloughs are too wet to be used as farmland.

Western sloughs are important to migrating waterfowl, providing a wet stopping-off point for the birds. This belies the general feeling that they exist only to provide a breeding ground for frogs and mosquitoes.

Slusher

A slusher was a horse-drawn bucket or scoop. It is a smaller version of the Fresno used for earthmoving on the farm. The flat-bottomed bucket was attached by chains to the horse's harness and was controlled by two wooden handles. A slusher was probably used to create the Digout (or Dugout).

Slyp/Slyping

Slyping was a method of haying in which the haystack was built in the field on a big, low sled and then hauled to its location. At the final location, the haystack was held by a canvas and rope girdle, which was staked to the ground while the sled was pulled out from underneath.

The term comes from the name of the sled on which the haystack was built. If the sled was used for hauling stones it was a STONEBOAT. When used for hauling hay it was a slyp.

Smudge

If mosquitoes, black flies, and NOSEEUMS are things of the West, then so is the smudge. A smudge is a smoky fire made to keep insects away. The only trouble is, if the smudge is smoky enough to keep the insects away, it is decidedly unpleasant for the humans as well.

Snard Lumps

This is the only term discovered for something that is so much a part of the Western winter existence that there must be many more terms for it, although most of them may be unprintable. A snard lump is the collection of ice and snow that builds up under the fender of a car in comparatively warm winter conditions. These snard lumps keep building up while you are driving and seldom fall off, unless kicked, until you park in your garage or parking space. There they immediately drop off and freeze in a solid lump behind each wheel!

Snatch Team

A snatch team was an extra team hooked to the front of the regular team to help pull the load or equipment out of a gravel pit or other difficult spot. Today, an extra train engine added for a steep grade, the extra cat added for the tough pull, is called a snatch engine.

Snirt

Snirt is an appropriately descriptive term for a unique prairie weather phenomenon. While it is not in the vocabulary of Environment Canada and, therefore, never heard in formal weather forecasting, snirt is a combination of snow and dirt. It occurs when strong winds drive snow over bare fields picking up dirt that becomes mixed with the snow.

Snowbirds

This is a term used in reference to Westerners, both by themselves and by others. Snowbirds are the prairie residents who head for the warmer weather of the southern United States during the winter months.

Most snowbirds are retired, although in times of prosperity there may be active grain farmers in the flock. But their numbers seldom include the rancher or mixed farmer, as one of the joys of animal husbandry is that it is a seven-days-a-week, fifty-two-weeks-a-year activity. You can only get away from livestock if someone else can take care of them.

Snow Lizards

Snow lizards are those little wisps of dry snow that blow about on the highway. Also known as snow snakes, these moving streaks of snow can be very distracting to tired drivers.

Snow Planes

Snow planes were propeller-driven sleighs that were a forerunner of the BOMBARDIER that would one day become a snowmobile. Snow planes resembled the marsh buggies that are in use today in places such as the Everglades in Florida, but featured an enclosed, rather than open, area ahead of the propeller.

Snow Snakes

See SNOW LIZARDS.

Snye

This is an interesting word that is also known in other parts of the country, where it refers to a small tributary of a river. However, it appears to have two distinctly prairie uses.
1. The old meandering rivers of the flat plains frequently cut off one of their looping bends to form what is properly called an oxbow, or dried-up river bend. Oxbows that fill with water in the spring, or at times of heavy runoff, but remain dry at other times, may be called snyes on the prairies.
2. The snye at Fort McMurray is one of two legs of the Clearwater River where it empties into the Athabasca River. Under normal conditions, the water flows out through both legs of the Clearwater River into the Athabasca, as if around an island in the Clearwater. However, under certain conditions of high water, the Athabasca River flows into one branch of the Clearwater and out the other, turning the land between the legs of that river into an island in the Athabasca, rather than an island in the Clearwater. The leg of the Clearwater River in which the flow of water is sometimes reversed is the snye.

Social

In Manitoba, it is almost mandatory for the friends of a bride and groom to hold a social prior to a wedding. Growing out of the parties that were associated with Ukrainian weddings, these socials have become a custom for everyone. A hall is rented, music booked, and tickets are sold to one and all. Profits from the ticket sales and from the bar, an essential part of the social, go to the bride and groom. In the larger centres especially, it is cheap entertainment with drink prices at a fraction of what would be paid in a bar or cocktail lounge. Young people flock to the myriad socials being held each Friday and Saturday night in halls ranging from church basements to community clubs. Once upon a time, you were expected to know the bride or groom, but not anymore. Your ticket to a social is a ticket to a cheap evening's entertainment.

A good social can net thousands of dollars for the wedding couple. They are so profitable that there have been reports of socials being run as commercial enterprises with a "duty couple" standing by to swear that they are getting married if a liquor inspector should check. But the permit required makes that impossible today.

While such parties are not unknown in other parts of the West, as well as other parts of the country, nowhere are they such an integral part of the young adult scene as they are in Manitoba, and nowhere else do they go by the name of socials.

Sod Buster

Sod buster is yet another term for the farmer, this one more descriptive and less insulting than many, as sod busting is a legitimate term.

Sod Busting

As the term suggests, sod busting was, and still is, the act of breaking virgin land for farming.

Soddie

The soddie was the sod shack the homesteader lived in until a cabin could be built. The sod was cut about fourteen inches wide and twenty-eight inches long. The walls of a soddie were then made twenty-eight inches, or two sod-widths thick, with every second layer of sod laid crosswise. Frequently, there were no windows because of the problems of framing them. Generally speaking, they were warm in the winter and cool in the summer, but they were also dark and dreary and were abandoned for a cabin as soon as possible.

Soddies could be built into a hill or partially buried, forming something that was half dugout, half soddie. The soddie could be roofed

with wood, which was often covered with dirt or sod. This could cause considerable discomfort in wet weather. Applicable expressions ranged from "Two days rain outside, four days rain inside," to "Two days rain outside, two weeks rain inside!" While the second of these may be a slight exaggeration, a sod roof did in fact keep out the rain for a couple of days and then the seepage began. The disheartening part was that when the rain finally stopped and the sun shone again it took several days for the roof to dry out and the dripping indoors to stop.
See also DUGOUT.

Sourdough

1. When yeast was hard to come by, the easiest way to keep baking leavened bread was with a sourdough starter, also called MOTHER YEAST. Sourdough is a mixture of yeast, water, flour, and sugar which is left to ferment for several days. After that, it can then be kept almost indefinitely if maintained at the correct temperature and replenished with equal amounts of flour and water each time a portion of it is used.
2. From their use of sourdough, the early pioneers and prospectors in the West and in the Yukon were known as sourdoughs. From this the term was sometimes used to indicate someone who had been in the area for some time, as opposed to the newcomer, or TENDERFOOT.

Sowing Wild Oats

This expression is now used far and wide, but it must have originated in farming country. Frequently used simply to mean having a wild time with wine, women, and song, the expression actually refers to loose sexual activity. Wild oats are the weeds that keep coming up in the legitimate crop, so promiscuous behaviour can result in illegitimate children springing up among the legitimate.

Spits

Many people love their sunflower seeds, but there is only one way to get rid of the shells. You can spit them demurely into your hand, you can spit them across the room, or you can spit them anywhere between those two extremes, but spit them you must. It was inevitable, then,

that sunflower seeds would become known as spits. See also
UKRAINIAN PEANUTS.

Sunflowers are grown as a crop in many areas of the West, but
Altona, Manitoba, calls itself the Sunflower Capital of Canada.

Spotting

Spotting is the placement of railway cars where they are needed, but the
first thought for prairie inhabitants will be the spotting of grain cars at
the ELEVATOR by the TRAMP engine that took away the filled cars and
spotted empties to be filled.

Stampede

While a stampede was originally, and still is for that matter, the wild,
headlong flight of a herd of frightened animals, the first association for
most people today would be the rodeo. Actually, the stampede is the
rodeo and all the other rides, games, and attractions that go with it.

The best known stampede is the Calgary Stampede, which is
recognized as the world's largest rodeo. The first Calgary Exhibition,
as it was then called, was conceived of in 1884 and first held in 1886.
In 1908 it became the Dominion Exposition, and in 1912 a Wild
West Extravaganza was added to create the Calgary Stampede. In
1930 the Calgary Industrial Exposition joined with the Stampede to
form the Calgary Exhibition and Stampede—now known universally
as the Calgary Stampede.

Stay

Western Canadians are often heard to say that they have stayed in a
certain town. This may be misleading to many as stay, in this case, does
not mean to spend some time, as in, "I stayed there last night." When a
Westerner says that he or she stayed there, it may well mean that he or
she lived there, as in, "I stayed there for fifteen years."

Stetson

Stetson is a trade name that became the generic name for the hat of the
West, especially among horsemen. When worn by a real cowboy, a
Stetson is not an affectation. A true Stetson is warm in winter and cool

in summer. It is water resistant and the wide brim serves as sunshade, umbrella, and windbreak.

Stockers

Stockers are young cattle bought as replacement cattle to replenish your stock. Stockers differ from FEEDERS in that feeders will only be held long enough to fatten for market, while stockers will be retained for breeding and the long-term development of the herd.

Stoneboat

A stoneboat is the sled used for hauling the stones off the farmland and for transporting other heavy objects. It is simply a wooden deck raised off the ground on runners just far enough to allow it to be dragged. The closer the deck can be kept to the ground, the less the rocks have to be lifted to place them on the platform.

The runners of the stoneboat were usually logs trimmed as smoothly as possible to reduce the considerable drag of the heavy sled in summer. The ice and snow of winter reduced that drag enough that high-spirited boys engaged in stoneboat races. These races were considered good country sport provided they took place within a mile or two of medical help, as the chance of bumps, bruises, and broken limbs was high. The driver had to stand on the stoneboat without any support and keep balanced, while controlling the team that was pulling the sled over rough terrain. If one runner snagged on an obstacle, throwing the stoneboat to one side, the driver's only hope was to leap off and run several paces in an attempt to regain balance and keep out of the path of the heavy, bouncing stoneboat.

Stook/Stooking

No longer seen, the stook was a teepee of sheaves. It allowed the wheat to remain upright, and therefore dry, until it was threshed. The field mice, however, assumed it was done to provide them with homes!

The making of the stooks, or stooking, is still remembered by some as one of the many back-breaking labours of farming in the early days. See also BUNCH OF BALES.

Stormstayed

This term did not originate on the prairies, or in Canada for that matter, but in usage it may be different enough to be worth comment. In most other places where the term is used, it is usually associated with the sea; the ship that cannot put to sea because of the storm being stormstayed. Obviously that does not fit on the prairies. For us to be stormstayed is to be snowbound—to be unable to leave home or to get home because of a blizzard, or because of the snow left by a storm.

Straight Combining

Straight combining is when the combine is used to cut and immediately thresh the grain, rather than to pick up a previously cut swath for threshing.

Strike out a Land

When you cut the first furrow in a large expanse of virgin land, you strike out a land. In order to get the first straight furrow, stakes could be set out or natural objects used as a sightline. While there is still some new land to be opened, most present-day farmers never have, and never will, open a field for the first time.

What an incredible experience it must have been for the first farmers who looked out on that vast expanse of unbroken prairie and set out to strike out a land. Occasionally the out was removed and the expression became to strike, or to strikes, a land.

Stripping

1. Stripping is the process of getting the last of the milk from the cow when milking by hand.
2. Stripping is also the longer process of drying up the milk cow before she starts producing for her own calf.

Strollers

Strollers are the rocks on the surface of farmland. These are the first to be picked when picking rocks, as they are the most visible and the easiest to remove. Strollers are one of the infamous trio STROLLERS, GRINNERS, and SLEEPERS.

Stubblejumper

Yet another slightly derogatory term for a homesteader or farmer, stubblejumper has become one of our Eastern friends' favourite names for Westerners.

Stumping

Stumping can either be pulling tree stumps, or to be out on the political hustings drumming up support for the next election. While stumping, as an electioneering term, goes back to the 1700s in the United States and is based on the use of a tree stump as a platform from which to speak, it became widely used in western Canada, where politicians out on the stump travelled from community to community with their political message.

Use of the term in the West is rather ironic since the BALD PRAIRIE supplied few stumps big enough for a politician to stand on. On the prairies, the platform was usually a piece of farm equipment. This has led to numerous stories, one of which is most frequently attributed to the Alberta Labour politician Bill Irvine, although it has been told many times using other names. Whether it was Bill Irvine or someone else, the most suitable platform from which to speak at one gathering turned out to be a manure spreader. He cheerfully climbed onto it and said, "Well, boys, this is the first time I have spoken from a Conservative platform!"

Stump Ranch

Stump ranch was the facetious term that servicemen from the prairies often used in reference to their farms back home when they were stationed in England during World War II. Many a war bride received quite a shock when she discovered the true nature of the stump ranch in western Canada.

Stupid Labour

Stupid labour refers to work associated with government make-work projects where the creation of jobs is more important than the product of the work. While the term could have come about all by itself, it is actually a deliberate corruption of another term. During the 1930s, unemployed men were given general labouring and construction work to do in order to pay off their taxes. This work was officially known as statute labour, but quickly became known as stupid labour.

Suckers
Newborn hogs are referred to as suckers for a fairly obvious reason.

Sucking the Hind Teat/Tit
This is not the crude expression that some might think it is. Less milk is generally available from the two hind teats than from those further forward on nursing animals such as pigs. Often it is the weakest of the young that get relegated to these, but even if there is some rotation, those on the hind teats at any given time are not getting as much as the others. As an expression, therefore, it means to bring up the rear, to be shortchanged, or not to be getting all that you could or should.

Sulky
A sulky, or sulkey, is not just the light carriage used in harness racing. It was a single-bottom plough, as opposed to the GANG PLOUGH.

Sunfishing
Sunfishing is a peculiar type of bucking in which an animal appears to be trying to twist upside down in the air as if it were fishing for sun on its belly. Broncs that tend to sunfish when being ridden in the rodeo are called sunfishers.

Supper
On the prairies, the noon meal was traditionally the biggest meal of the day, and was called DINNER. That has meant that the evening meal, usually called dinner elsewhere, is known as supper.

Survey
For details of the Western survey, see DOMINION LANDS SURVEY.

Swather

The swather is the machine that cuts a band of grain and lays it in a narrow row, or swath. The swath will later be picked up by the combine for threshing. The bigger the swather, the wider the swath it cuts. See also CUT A WIDE SWATH.

Sweetgrass

Sweetgrass is a name applied across North America to a large variety of sweet-smelling grasses. It also refers to the prairie grasses that are burned by aboriginals as part of their religious or spiritual ceremonies.

Prior to the North American Aboriginal Games in Winnipeg in 2002, border guards at all ports of entry, especially those in Manitoba, were given special instruction on sweetgrass so that American aboriginals on their way to the Games would not be accused of trying to bring illegal substances into the country.

T

As in

Tiny, Saskatchewan;
Tidal, Manitoba;
Tilley, Alberta

Take to the Meat House

As the meat house refers to the abattoir or slaughterhouse, to take someone to the meat house is a variation on the common exaggerated threat to kill someone when a little more than displeased with their actions, as in "I'll take you to the meat house if you do that again."

Tank Heater

A tank heater is used to heat the water trough in winter so that animals can be watered outdoors in very cold weather.

Tarpoleon

In many areas of the West, things that are stored outdoors are covered with a big canvas or plastic tarpoleon, pronounced tar po'le on, to provide protection from the weather. In other parts of the country they tend, for some inexplicable reason, to pronounce it as it is spelled—tarpaulin.

Tenderfoot

A tenderfoot is a newcomer to the West who has not, as yet, learned the ways of his or her new home.

Texas Gate

This is another name for a cattle crossing, a term that originated in another part of the continent but which is widely used in western Canada. See also CATTLE CROSSING.

Thatcher Patchers

During the days of Ross Thatcher, Premier of Saskatchewan from 1964 to 1971, workers doing repairs to Saskatchewan highways were known as Thatcher patchers. This is not just a clever rhyming term for the workers; it was a sarcastic comment on the condition of Saskatchewan highways and the blame placed on politicians.

Thatcher Wagon

At one time, also during the days of Premier Thatcher, the Saskatchewan government ruled that pickup trucks were eligible as farm vehicles and could use purple gas. This allowed people to cut away the back of their cars to form a type of pickup truck that qualified for purple gas. This strange vehicle was quickly dubbed a Thatcher wagon.

The Coast

The Coast, to a western Canadian, is the Pacific coast. The Atlantic coast would be called the East Coast or the Maritimes. See also CENTRAL CANADA.

Thistle Tramper

Thistle trampers are children. During the 1930s, the abundant thistle was used for cattle feed, but it was first trampled down and salted to soften the prickles, a job performed by the children of the family. It is said that many families announced the arrival of new offspring by stating that a new thistle tramper had arrived.

Thrashing

Thrashing is what the western farmer is doing when separating the grain from the chaff. Farmers elsewhere do the same thing, but they usually pronounce it the way it is properly spelled—threshing.

The pronunciation of the word as thrashing is so pervasive that you will find it spelled that way in all kinds of writing. It is interesting to read books about the settlement of western Canada containing pictures of the old threshing gangs, across the bottom of which is often written something like, "Thrashing gang on Charlie's farm."

Through the Windshield

Through the windshield is the third way to get thrown off a horse, the other two being OUT THE SIDE DOOR and OUT THE BACK DOOR. To be thrown through the windshield is, of course, to be thrown over the horse's head.

Throw In/Throw Back the Ridge

As noted under DEAD FURROW, when ploughing with a one-way plough, the first furrow turned the earth over onto the surface of the ground, rather than into an adjacent furrow, forming a ridge. To plough that ridge in the opposite direction, in order to level the land, was to throw in the ridge, or throw back the ridge.

Any action undertaken to square off an old debt or injustice, therefore, is done to throw in or throw back the ridge. When used figuratively like this, it simply means to smooth things out again.

Tie Yard

In the horse and buggy days, many towns provided a tie yard that was an area fenced on three sides with hitching rails. When a farmer arrived in town he could drive into the tie yard, tie up his harnessed team, throw down some hay, and go off to do his business. The teenaged boys in town were not averse, on occasion, to borrowing a team from the tie yard for a short ride in the country—an early form of joy riding. Occasionally a farmer arrived back at the tie yard to find his horses tied where he had left them, munching their hay, but in a sweat after they should have been standing for two hours.

Tighter than a Cow's Ass at Fly Time

This expression means very tight indeed, as anyone knows who has seen old Bossy suffering through fly season. Actually, it is not all that funny. When flies are very bad, animals can literally be driven mad. If you have ever been out in the bush when the black flies, mosquitoes and NOSEEUMS were all swarming, you know how close you can come to being rendered a babbling idiot. As well as keeping their body orifices tightly closed, animals, including the mighty buffalo, will sometimes coat themselves with mud as a protection against flying insects.

Toad Bellies

Toad bellies is a name given to deep-fried chunks of dough. When deep-frying other foods in batter, pieces of the batter that drip off and fry by themselves qualify for the name, as do pieces of actual bread or bun dough that are dropped into the deep-fryer.

Toad Stabber

Your toad stabber is your pocketknife, if it is the right kind. Originally, the toad stabber was the spike, properly called a marlinspike, on pocketknives so equipped. After a while the name came to stand for the whole pocketknife when it had such a spike. Toad stabbing was precisely what some boys did with that marlinspike. After all, they did not often have to use it for its real purpose, wire and rope splicing.

Too Dead to be Buried

This is a wonderfully appropriate expression to describe a carcass that is found in an advanced state of decay. Originating in range country where it described stock found dead and decaying, the expression has spread and can now be applied to any carcass, animal of course, that is found in this condition.

The expression can also be used for things that are figuratively dead. So, if your business or your marriage is too dead to be buried, there is absolutely no hope of reviving it.

Took a Homestead

When someone took a homestead, it may not have been under the terms of the Homestead Act. He may have been thrown from his horse and have laid claim to a patch of land face first! See also BUY A HOMESTEAD.

Too Thick to Drink, Too Thin to Plough

This expression was first used to describe the Mississippi River, but it had a certain appeal to the Western farmer who tended to use it when unsure of how to handle a situation. After all, if you can't drink it or plough it, what on earth are you going to do with it? This is not to be confused with TOO WET TO PLOUGH.

Too Wet to Plough

Obviously, when it is raining there comes a time when you can no longer work the land because it is literally too wet to plough. When his wife or daughter is in tears, the man of the house may declare that if the tears keep up it will soon be too wet to plough.

Toronto Couch

The Toronto couch is a couch with a lower shelf that pulls out to make a bed. In an interesting play on regional expressions, what is a Toronto couch in the West is called a Winnipeg couch or Calgary couch in the East.

Towns

Prairie towns are not always the group of houses and shops that grew up around the country elevator. A town is the proper name for a colony of prairie dogs. Unchecked prairie dog towns can totally destroy a field. See also PRAIRIE DOG.

Township

The township is the largest unit of the Western survey. It is an area of land six miles by six miles that is divided into thirty-six sections. Townships are identified by their number north from the forty-ninth parallel, or the Canada-US border, and by their particular range measured east or west of the Prime Meridian or west of meridians one through six. See also DOMINION LANDS SURVEY.

Tractor Cap

What others would call a ball cap the farmer calls a tractor cap, especially if the logo on it is that of a grain company, equipment dealer, fertilizer brand, or something else to do with farming.

This brings to mind the day an Eastern reporter was interviewing a Western farmer in 1969 or 1970. It was another of the many desperate times on prairie farms, and Otto Lang, federal minister in charge of the Canadian Wheat Board, was taking much of the heat. The reporter noticed the word POOL on the farmer's tractor cap and asked what it stood for. Without hesitation the farmer replied, "Piss On Otto Lang."

Tramp

The tramp was a train locomotive, or locomotives, that took away the loaded grain cars and SPOTTED empty cars in position to be filled at the ELEVATOR. Tramps were known by the area they worked. For example, the tramp out of Weyburn and working that area was the Weyburn tramp.

Transcona Depot

There is no depot or train station in the railway yards at Transcona, now part of Winnipeg, but it was the place where those who were riding the rails caught a freight train headed east or got off one arriving from the East. Therefore, during the Dirty Thirties when so many men were travelling this way, the Transcona yard became known as the Transcona Depot. See also McPHILLIPS STREET STATION.

Trash

Trash is not the garbage that has to be hauled out of the kitchen. It is the mixture of straw, chaff, and a little grain that is thrown out the back of a combine. The amount of grain in the trash will depend on various settings, the condition of the combine, and the rate at which the farmer is working. If you see a farmer catching some of the trash, he is checking it to see if the amount of grain escaping is acceptable for the rate at which he is working.

Trudeau Acres

Trudeau acres, or Trudeau's acres, are hectares. Taken to the extremes that it was, metrification was not exactly popular across the prairies. Having no concept of the extent to which the West is rooted in the imperial system by the terms of the land survey, Eastern politicians decided that what was acceptable to them must be acceptable to everyone.

Truska Riggin

Truska riggin was what the new Swedish immigrants called a threshing machine. This obviously anglicized version of a Swedish term appears to have been widely used in southern Alberta.

Tube Steak

While it is now widely applied to wieners, in Winnipeg tube steak originally referred to bologna. See also NORTH END ROUND.

Tumbleweed

The name tumbleweed does not just apply to the Russian thistle and other similar weeds that spread their seeds by breaking off and blowing about in the wind. The term may also be applied to the person who is always on the move, never putting down roots. See also SADDLE TRAMP.

Turkey Dumb

To be turkey dumb is to be really dense. Farmers generally consider turkeys to be about the most stupid creatures in the barnyard. However, turkey dumb is not quite as dumb as DUMB AS A SACK OF HAMMERS.

Two and a Juice

Draft beer in the beer parlour is always ordered with the call of DRAW TWO. If you want tomato juice as well in order to make redeye, the cry is TWO AND A JUICE. See also CALGARY REDEYE.

Two Pumpkins in a Sack

This is a rural description of the view of someone's too-large rear end in too-tight jeans, a view that has also been described as two pigs in a sack or, even worse, two pigs fighting in a sack.

As in

Underhill, Manitoba; Usona, Alberta; Unity, Saskatchewan

Ugly Enough to Knock a Dog off a Gut Wagon

As the GUT WAGON was the wagon carrying entrails and other waste away from the abattoir or slaughter house, it held a certain attraction for dogs. Helen of Troy had a face that launched a thousand ships. You can only imagine the degree of ugliness of the face required to knock a dog off a gut wagon!

Ukrainian Peanuts

Sunflower seeds are an immensely popular, habit-forming snack on the prairies. Perhaps as an attempt to place blame for the addiction elsewhere, in places where the ethnic background is largely Ukrainian, the sunflower seeds are called Ukrainian peanuts. They are also known as Russian peanuts in places where that is the predominant ethnic background.

Another name for them is SPITS, which makes sense to anyone who eats the seeds or has seen the trail of shells behind a sunflower seed eater.

Useless as Teats on a Bull/Boar/Fish

Whether given as teats or tits, these expressions are not as sexist or crude as one might first believe. The nursing of young animals is a fact of life on the farm and the various parts of animal anatomy are part of the normal vocabulary. Obviously, teats on a bull or boar would be totally useless, and therein lies the meaning of these expressions. See also LOOKING UP A DEAD HORSE'S ASS.

As in

Vulcan, Alberta;
Vonda, Saskatchewan;
Vista, Manitoba

Venarterte

While well known in areas of the West with large Icelandic populations, this Icelandic dish, with mid-European variations both in recipe and spelling, is seldom heard of elsewhere in Canada. It is a delicious cake with seven to ten thin shortbread-like layers separated by a prune-based filling. It may or may not be iced. In one variation, the prune filling is alternated with another made of apricots.

Vico

In an example of a trade name becoming the generic term for the product, chocolate milk in Saskatchewan is often simply called Vico. As with the Winnipeger who orders a nip in Regina, the Regina resident who orders Vico in Winnipeg will be met with a blank stare.

Volunteer Crop

A volunteer crop is one that grows from seeds scattered by the wind or left behind by the harvesting process. It may also be the crop of an annual plant that grows the following year without being deliberately planted.

In the debate over genetically modified crops, the possibility of genetically modified plants growing as a volunteer crop among unmodified plants is of concern to many farmers and grain exporters.

It is not just a case of a mixture of seed that contaminates a supposedly genetically unmodified field and jeopardizes sales to a number of countries. Genetically modified seed can only be grown by those who have purchased a licence to do so from the producer of the seed. Too heavy a concentration of modified crop on the field of an unlicensed farmer could lead to charges being laid. See also CATCH CROP.

As in

Wilkie, Saskatchewan; Waskada, Manitoba; Wild Horse, Alberta

Wannigans

Wannigans are either heavy felt boots worn in the winter, or the removable heavy felt liners for winter boots. Either way, they are felt footwear for cold weather.

Warsh

This is a very common word—after all, don't you warsh your face every morning? Like so many odd pronunciations, this one is dying out, but many Western residents, even if they don't pronounce it that way themselves, can remember the days of warshcloths and warshdays.

Washboard

Washboard (or warshboard) is not just the thing that was used to get the laundry clean. It is also a section of dirt or gravel road that has developed ripples across it like the ridges of an actual washboard. The gravel roads are routinely dragged by the PATROL to remove the washboard, but it never seems to help very much.

Water Belly

Water belly is the common term for a condition that occurs when cattle suffer from a water blockage.

Welcome as Hail and 'Hoppers

Two of the many horrors that can rob a farmer of all he has worked for are a hailstorm or an infestation of grasshoppers. Therefore, to be as welcome as hail and 'hoppers is to be not very welcome at all.

The only thing less welcome than hail and 'hoppers these days is the arrival of the auctioneer when the farm has gone bankrupt.

Welfare Cheque

When a farmer delivers his crop to the Canadian Wheat Board, he only gets a partial payment for the delivery. There will be interim and full payments made to him later, based on the final selling price of that year's crop to Canada's many customers. When the amount of these interim and final payments are determined, the federal government announces the million-dollar total payment as if it were some great magnanimous government handout to the farmers, instead of the final installment for their previously delivered goods. These payments, therefore, tend to be referred to as welfare cheques, as this would seem to be how Ottawa would like the rest of the country to view them.

There is a fair note of bitterness in the expression, especially if Ottawa then justifies a huge handout of general taxpayers' money to Ontario or Quebec on the basis that the West just received millions in a final wheat payment.

Final payments should not be confused with wheat subsidies, which are a form of assistance paid to farmers when the international price of wheat is too low to cover the cost of production.

Well

When a bull starts spinning around in a circle while bucking, the centre area around which he is spinning is known as the well. It is the most dangerous place that the rodeo cowboy can be thrown.

Well Hooked Up

Originating in the days of harnessing teams, something well hooked up had good-looking horses and good-looking harness and presented the epitome of a good-looking team. The phrase has, therefore, many associations with things that are well done or attractive. A person can be well hooked up, as having married money or prestige, or they can be well hooked up meaning good-looking and well dressed.

Wellington-Boot-Throwing Championship

Of all the contests and gimmicks used to attract attention to the local fair or exhibition, mention must be made of the Canadian Wellington-Boot-Throwing Championship, held annually at the Springfield Agricultural Fair in Dugald, Manitoba.

If you want to practise for the event, the Wellington is a size 8 rubber boot. All contestants throw the boot provided, so don't start melting lead to pour into the toe of an old size 8 boot! You will have to throw pretty close to 150 feet to set a new Canadian record.

As you may have noticed from tourist ads from the UK, Wellington-boot-throwing originated in that part of the world.

We've Howdied But We Haven't Shook

This lovely old Western expression means just about what it says: "We have said 'hello,' but we haven't shaken hands." In other words, we know each other by sight, but we really haven't met formally.

Whiskey Jack

Whiskey Jack is the name given to the beautiful bird properly known as the grey jay or Canada jay (*Perisoreus canadensis*). This name is said to come from the Indian word *wiss-ka-tjon*, or *wis-ka-chon*, which English speakers turned into whiskey John.

Wildcat

A wildcat is an oil well that is being drilled in an area where there have been no discoveries—that makes wildcatting it a high-risk venture. If a wildcat comes in, a new field has been discovered and, at one time anyway, fortunes might have been made. From this meaning in the oil patch, the term is sometimes transferred to any high-risk venture.

Winnipeg Couch

See Toronto Couch.

Winnipeg Forecast

A Winnipeg forecast is a weather forecast that, like so many weather forecasts, is not particularly accurate. The expression comes from Saskatchewan, and originated when the weather forecasting office in Regina was closed. That meant that weather forecasts for Saskatchewan now had to come out of Winnipeg. When you couple the generally bad reputation of weather forecasts with the resentment that they had to come from another province, you get a Winnipeg forecast. See also CBC Sunshine.

Winnipeg Meridian

The Winnipeg Meridian is another name for the Prime Meridian, the meridian from which the layout of ranges began for the survey of the West. See also Dominion Lands Survey.

Wolf Willow

The wolf willow (*Elaeagnus commutata*) is a shrub of the oleaster family. It has silver leaves with a silver and yellow flower. The fruit is edible, but not very tasty. A Canadian native plant, it is seldom seen anywhere but on the prairies.

Wrangler

A wrangler is one of the many terms for the cowboy who works with horses for an Outfit.

Wrinkly

Wrinkly is an old Western term implying age and short temper, not physical wrinkles, as one might think. If someone is getting wrinkly, he or she is getting hard to deal with and cantankerous. You can, therefore, get wrinkly before your time and before you are actually wrinkled.

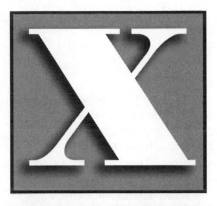

As in

Zoda, Manitoba; Youngstone, Alberta; Zealandia, Saskatchewan

Anyone who has ever checked through the final pages of a dictionary, or tried to get rid of the Xs and Zs in a Scrabble game, is aware of how thin the XYZ section of the dictionary can be. Prairie phrases beginning with these letters are equally limited. Only one is offered.

Young Heifer

Young heifer is really a redundant expression, as a HEIFER is a young cow that has not been bred, but the expression is heard nonetheless. So, let's just say that that it is a young, young cow.

FIFTH HOUSE

ABOUT FIFTH HOUSE BOOKS

FIFTH HOUSE PUBLISHERS, a Fitzhenry & Whiteside company, is a proudly western-Canadian press. Our publishing specialty is non-fiction, as we believe that every community must possess a positive understanding of its worth and place if it is to remain vital and progressive. FIFTH HOUSE is committed to "bringing the West to the rest" by publishing approximately twenty books a year about the land and people who make this region unique. Our books are selected for their quality, saleability, and contribution to the understanding of Western Canadian (and Canadian) history, culture, and environment.

Look for these books about prairie life from FIFTH HOUSE at your favourite bookstore.

Alberta Originals: Stories of Albertans Who Made a Difference,
    Brian Brennan, $16.95
Aunt Mary in the Granary and Other Prairie Stories, Eileen Comstock, $14.95
Barns of Western Canada, Bob Hainstock, $16.95
Building a Province: 60 Alberta Lives, Brian Brennan, $14.95
But It's a Dry Cold! Weathering the Canadian Prairies, Elaine Wheaton, $18.95
Country Calls: Memories of a Small-town Doctor, Dr. Sid Cornish with
    Judith Cornish, $14.95
Eternal Prairie: Exploring Rural Cemeteries of the West, R. Adams, $16.00
Five Pennies: A Prairie Boy's Story, Irene Morck, $14.95
Gateway City: Stories from Edmonton's Past, Alex Mair, $16.95
The Good Land: Stories of Saskatchewan People, Peter Wilson, $14.95
Gully Farm: A Story of Homesteading on the Canadian Prairies,
    Mary Hiemstra, $14.95
The Last Buffalo Hunter, Mary Weekes, $14.95
The Middle of Nowhere: Rediscovering Saskatchewan, Dennis Gruending, $16.95
No Spring Chicken: Thoughts on a Life Well Lived, Eileen Comstock, $16.95
Out of the Flames: Fires and Fire Fighting on the Canadian Prairies,
    Faye Reineberg Holt, $8.95
Scoundrels and Scallywags: Characters from Alberta's Past, Brian Brennan, $16.95
Sunny Side Up: Fond Memories of Prairie Life in the 1930s,
    Eileen Comstock, $16.95
What's in a Name: The Story of Saskatchewan Place Names, E.T. Russell, $14.95
Where the River Runs: Stories of the Saskatchewan and the People Drawn to
    Its Shores, Victor Carl Friesen, $21.95